Cambridge Elements ≡

Elements in the Archaeology of Europe
edited by
Manuel Fernández-Götz
University of Edinburgh
Bettina Arnold
University of Wisconsin–Milwaukee

SALT

White Gold in Early Europe

Anthony Harding
University of Exeter

E A A | European Association
of Archaeologists

CAMBRIDGE
UNIVERSITY PRESS

CAMBRIDGE
UNIVERSITY PRESS

University Printing House, Cambridge CB2 8BS, United Kingdom

One Liberty Plaza, 20th Floor, New York, NY 10006, USA

477 Williamstown Road, Port Melbourne, VIC 3207, Australia

314–321, 3rd Floor, Plot 3, Splendor Forum, Jasola District Centre,
New Delhi – 110025, India

103 Penang Road, #05–06/07, Visioncrest Commercial, Singapore 238467

Cambridge University Press is part of the University of Cambridge.

It furthers the University's mission by disseminating knowledge in the pursuit of
education, learning, and research at the highest international levels of excellence.

www.cambridge.org
Information on this title: www.cambridge.org/9781009017640
DOI: 10.1017/9781009038973

First published 2021

A catalogue record for this publication is available from the British Library.

ISBN 978-1-009-01764-0 Paperback
ISSN 2632-7058 (online)
ISSN 2632-704X (print)

Salt

White Gold in Early Europe

Elements in the Archaeology of Europe

DOI: 10.1017/9781009038973
First published online: July 2021

Anthony Harding
University of Exeter

Author for correspondence: Anthony Harding, A.F.Harding@exeter.ac.uk

Abstract: This Element provides a concise account of the archaeology of salt production in ancient Europe. It describes what salt is, where it is found, what it is used for, and its importance for human and animal health. The different periods of the past in which it was produced are described, from earliest times down to the medieval period. Attention is paid to the abundant literary sources that inform us about salt in the Greek and Roman world, as well as the likely locations of production in the Mediterranean and beyond. The economic and social importance of salt in human societies means that salt has served as a crucial aspect of trade and exchange over the centuries, and potentially as a means of individuals and societies achieving wealth and status.

Keywords: salt, ancient Europe, briquetage, solar evaporation, trough technique

ISBNs: 9781009017640 (PB), 9781009038973 (OC)
ISSNs: 2632-7058 (online), 2632-704X (print)

Contents

1 Introduction

Salt, sodium chloride, is such a common substance in our lives that we tend to take it for granted. A trip to the supermarket allows us to choose between several different sorts – sea salt, rock salt, cooking salt (with added iodine); factory-processed salt, artisanal salt; home-produced salt, salt imported from the other side of the globe. Most of the time we pay no attention to it, nor do we think about where it comes from. It is just there in our lives. But it was not always thus.

Some ancient authors wrote about salt, but they generally tell us less than we would like to know about where salt came from and how it was produced. This suggests that for them too it was such a common commodity that they did not think it worth going into details. Medieval and Renaissance writers are more forthcoming, notably Georgius Agricola, writing in the sixteenth century; from them it is possible to infer much of what went before them. In fact, the production of salt was a major concern at all periods of the past, including the ancient past. In this Element, I shall describe what we know of the European production of salt from earliest times down to the Roman period.

The Importance of Salt

Humans and animals all need to consume salt in order to get an intake of sodium, which regulates the fluid balance of the body and assists with other functions of the internal organs. The fact that for many people salt adds 'savour' to food, in other words it makes bland food taste more interesting, is perhaps a fortunate stimulus to its consumption, if not a biological adaptation. How much salt is necessary for health is a matter of some debate: the figure of 6 g daily (2.4 g of sodium) is often quoted as the ideal maximum (it is the amount recommended by the NHS in Britain, for instance); larger amounts are believed to increase the risks for high blood pressure, cardiovascular disease and other problems. Eating too little salt also causes problems, though in fact most humans get enough salt through their normal diet, especially if they eat meat, eggs or fish. Animals will seek out salt if not given it as part of their diet. Experimental work in the 1960s and 70s showed how animals deprived of salt suffer ill effects that lead to poor health; sodium is needed especially for nursing young animals. This 'hunger for salt' (Denton 1984) makes animals seek out salty pools or rocks to lick, and to eat vegetation that is rich in sodium.

Salt is also crucial for other reasons, the most significant in pre-industrial societies being the preservation of food. Its antibacterial properties make it ideal for this purpose, as well as for combating infection from wounds and sores. In peasant communities it is used to this day to treat health problems such as rheumatism and arthritis. Today, however, in most of the world the uses of salt as a foodstuff and preservative are dwarfed by those of industry and road-salting in winter, which do not apply to times before the Industrial Revolution.

Salt in the World

Salt is found commonly in the world. The largest deposits are in the Americas, Saharan Africa and parts of Asia (China and the Himalayan area); the largest producers today are China, the United States and India. In Europe, the largest producer is Germany, but several other countries have significant salt resources, notably Spain, Poland, Romania and the UK (salt is one of the few natural resources in which Britain is self-sufficient).

Much has been written about historical salt exploitation in North America and in China, while ethnographic accounts have covered Niger (Gouletquer 1975; Gouletquer & Kleinmann 1984), New Guinea (Godelier 1969; Pétrequin *et al.* 2000) and several Mesoamerican countries (Good 1995; Williams 1999). Several books and websites give excellent descriptions and images of non-industrial salt

Figure 1 Blocks of Taoudenni salt at the port of Mopti in Mali, Africa (information in accompanying text and this image 'Mopti sel' by Taguelmoust downloaded at the French language Wikipedia. Licensed under CC BY-SA 3.0 via Wikimedia Commons - http://commons.wikimedia.org/wiki/File:Mopti_sel .jpg#/media/File:Mopti_sel.jpg).

production, for instance in Mali (Figure 1) (www.saltworkconsultants.com /ancient-salt-trade-and-its-value/, last accessed 14 December 2020).

In this volume my aim is to provide a short account of salt production in the ancient world, concentrating on Europe from earliest times down to the Roman period. Good accounts of salt in parts of the Americas are those by Ian Brown, Heather McKillop and Dumas & Eubanks (Brown 1981; McKillop 2002; Dumas & Eubanks 2021), while for China the best accounts in English are those by Tora Yoshida and Rowan Flad (Yoshida 1993; Flad 2011). For Africa the accounts by Paul Lovejoy (1986) and Ann McDougall's many contributions are important; there is a useful web article by Mark Cartwright on the west African salt trade (www.ancient.eu/article/1342/the-salt-trade-of-ancient-west-africa/, last accessed 10 November 2020).[1]

There are several histories of salt production and consumption (e.g. Mollat 1968; Multhauf 1978; Bergier 1982; Adshead 1992; Kurlansky 2002) and several important books by the historian Jean-Claude Hocquet (e.g. Hocquet 1978–9; 2001; 2019). His 2001 book is an excellent introduction to the theme, with marvellous photographs of salt production in many parts of the world.

The story in Europe goes back millennia, and in technological terms is varied and often complex. In the sections that follow I shall look at these matters in detail.

2 What Salt Is, Where It Occurs and How It Is Exploited

Sodium chloride, common salt, is an evaporite mineral, that is, one that is concentrated or crystallised from an aqueous solution, either the oceans, or lakes such as the Dead Sea or the Great Salt Lake in Utah. Through evaporation, over geological timescales, rock salt (halite) is created. Salt in rock form is found in the form of diapirs, dome-like structures arising from ancient seawater deposits, protruding upwards and sometimes appearing on the earth's surface. In mountainous areas, these domes have been subjected to various tectonic processes that have resulted in them being uplifted, so that the salt rock appears at or near the surface. The presence of underground diapirs is also responsible for the emergence of salt-water springs that emerge into the light of day without any rock salt being apparent, as rainwater and other underground water is forced upwards.

Salt is found widely in the world. In this Element, I am concerned principally with Europe, where salt occurs in many areas (Figure 2). The largest area is that spreading across the north of the continent, from northern England through Germany and Poland, but there are many other areas that are rich in deposits,

---

[1] These are only a few of the many books and articles on salt in different parts of the world.

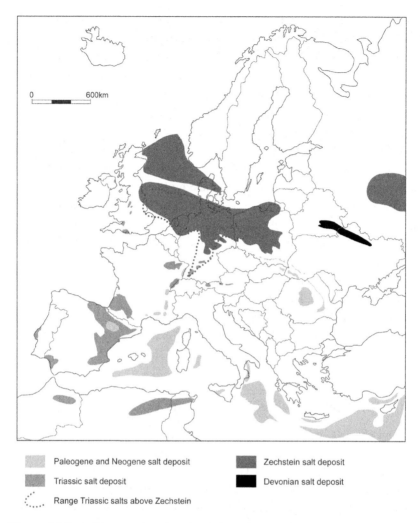

Figure 2 Map of Europe showing the major salt areas and their geological age.
Source: Harding 2014.

notably the Carpathian area, where the 'foredeep' extends from southern Poland
through western Ukraine, touching on northern Romania. Another area with
many salt deposits occurs in the Alps, particularly in Austria; also in France,
Spain, Turkey and elsewhere. Of course concentrating on rock salt and inland
salt-water springs ignores the other main source of salt: the sea. The salt content
of seawater is typically around 3.5 per cent (i.e. 35 g of salt in 1 litre of water);
extracting it through evaporation is crucial for coastal communities, in the past
as nowadays. Salt lakes can contain much more salt: the Dead Sea, for instance,

is around 340 g/l saline, the Great Salt Lake of Turkey (Tuz Gölü) up to 324 g/l, compared with the Adriatic at 33 g/l, or the Black Sea at only 18 g/l.

Although Europe as a whole is rich in salt, individual parts of it are not. This is very significant in historical and economic terms, since it means that those parts with no access to salt had to obtain it from neighbouring or more distant areas.

Exploitation of Salt Sources

Salt may be produced in a number of different ways, most of which were utilised in prehistoric Europe. Which method was used will have depended on the nature of the deposit to be exploited.

In general, salt is obtained either by mining and quarrying or through the evaporation of saline liquids (brine or seawater). Most forms of exploitation in antiquity utilised one or other of these forms of salt: as Pliny the Elder said, 'all salt is artificial or native', the distinction between *sal nativus* (rock salt) and *sal facticius* (salt obtained through human action). It is also possible to obtain salt from halophyte plants (plants that tolerate salty conditions, found growing on salty soils), which can be burnt on a fire and the salt crystals picked off. Salty mud or marsh can also be used, through a process of filtration or leaching known as lixiviation. Archaeologically speaking, both the extraction of rock salt and the boiling of salt water leave clear traces in the archaeological record. The burning of plants is not visible archaeologically, but may be assumed to have happened, since it is well known in ethnographic situations.

Quarrying and Mining

The simplest method in technological terms, in the case where rock salt outcrops on the surface, is simply to break lumps of salt off the rock body. This involves no equipment other than strong hammers. This is, however, somewhat easier said than done. The rock surface may be very hard – indeed, if it occurs on the earth's surface, it is bound to be, as otherwise it would dissolve and wash away through weathering.

Where rock salt outcrops on the earth's surface, it would be natural for ancient people to exploit it, since it can be used with little manipulation; it can be ground down to a form that can be used directly, or it can be dissolved in water and then evaporated using heat to produce salt in crystalline form. In practice, there are rather few known locations in Europe where rock salt was exploited directly; either because there are few such outcrops easily detectable or because the rock is extremely hard, making working it time-consuming and laborious, or both. Instead it is the exploitation of brine springs and streams, or of seawater, that accounts for the largest amount of evidence for salt production from the ancient world.

In prehistoric times, the extraction of salt in rock form is known above all from the great mining sites of Hallstatt and Hallein in Austria, though there are other locations in the German and Austrian Alps where salt is present, for instance Bad Reichenhall in Bavaria or Hall in Tirol in Austria. Even there, the method of exploitation does not only involve the extraction of hard rock, as I shall discuss in the following. There are many parts of modern Romania, especially in Moldavia and Muntenia (the eastern and south-eastern provinces of that country) where salt can be seen outcropping in great massifs (Figure 3). It would seem inconceivable that such outcrops were not exploited in ancient times, but since they continue to be exploited on a small scale to the present day, any trace of ancient activity has been lost.

Modern rock salt mines are deep, far deeper than would have been technologically possible in prehistory. One can visit such places in parts of Germany, Poland, Romania and Spain; nowadays one is transported down many tens of metres in lifts, which brings home the impossibility of such processes being possible in ancient times. Instead, the rock would have been worked from the surface, in effect in a form of quarrying. The Romans, by contrast, developed sophisticated techniques for deep mining, using a range of technologies for

Figure 3 Rock salt at Bisoca, Muntenia, Romania.

Photo: author.

pumping out water and providing means of getting miners in and mined material out. These are best known from Spain in the context of metal extraction, but there is evidence for their use in the province of Dacia too.

Rock salt is hard, so that extracting it with pre-industrial technology is a significant obstacle. My own experience in dealing with rock salt in fieldwork in Romania shows how hard the rock may be and how laborious breaking it up is. I have seen local people working with heavy iron hammers and picks on outcrops in Buzău county in Muntenia (specifically in the area around Bisoca and Mânzăleşti), getting lumps of rock to provide salt lick for their animals; and a colleague, Andrea Chiricescu, working at the time for the Museum of the Eastern Carpathians in Sf. Gheorghe, filmed a man working a rock surface at the village of Dumitra near Bistriţa in the north of Transylvania. He was using a heavy iron pick to strike the rock surface, but it took him fifteen minutes to remove a block of salt a few kilos in weight (plus numerous small chips). On another occasion, at the site of excavations at Băile Figa near Beclean in the same county, a bulldozer which was being used to remove the overburden could only scratch the surface of the rock salt with the teeth of its bucket.

The implications for the prehistoric exploitation of rock salt are obvious: suitable hard stones (or, in later times, bronze or iron picks and hammers) must have been used, presumably mounted firmly onto hafts and secured with bindings of leather or fibrous vegetable matter (clematis or similar). It must, however, have been a long and tedious process to get any reasonable quantity of rock – which would then need to be processed by grinding or dissolving and re-evaporating.

In general, one might presume that wherever rock salt appeared on the surface, people would have wished to exploit it. Archaeologically speaking, this presents a difficulty, in that such working is most unlikely to leave any traces. Only the presence of suitable hammers or grinding stones might indicate the existence of such work. But this is to ignore some of the most important and prolific sites where rock salt exploitation took place: the mining sites of the Austrian Alps, above all Hallstatt and the Dürrnberg near Hallein.

Hallstatt, which has been subject of extensive investigation in recent years, is rightly regarded as one of the most important salt production sites in prehistoric Europe. The extensive workings lie alongside an upland valley on the Plassen mountain above the eponymous lake (Figure 4), and are adjacent to the famous Iron Age cemetery whose contents gave their name to the period between *c.*1200 and 700 BC. The different parts of the mining area belong to different periods; the Bronze Age workings are mainly in the northern area, while in the eastern and western areas the remains belong to the early Iron Age. In both, it was necessary to engage in deep mining, cutting shafts and adits to create tunnels into the mountain.

Figure 4 Aerial view of Lake Hallstatt, showing the town and the plateau where
the Iron Age cemetery and salt mine are located.

Photo: courtesy of Luftbildarchiv/Institut für Ur- und Frühgeschichte Wien.

At the working surface, the miners used picks to extract the rock. The precise
technique adopted differed remarkably between the Bronze and the Iron Age. In
the Bronze Age, deep parallel grooves were hacked into the rock surface and the
intermediate material hammered out in lumps or chips. In the Iron Age, the picks
were used to create heart-shaped blocks which were removed whole, with as little
waste as possible. In both cases, the rock was moved from the working surface for
further processing; in medieval and modern times this principally means dissolving
the salt in water and evaporating it, with the aim of removing the unwanted
minerals in the salt, which precipitate at different stages in the evaporation process.

Recent work has, however, shown that there is a less strenuous way to extract
chunks of salt from a rock surface. This involves the use of wooden troughs, as
described in the next section. Experimental work by Dan Buzea from the National
Museum of the Eastern Carpathians in Sf. Gheorghe (south-east Transylvania)
has shown that by letting fresh water drip from a perforated trough onto a rock salt
surface for some hours, depressions where the salt has dissolved are produced
(Buzea 2010; 2013) (Figure 5A). A series of such depressions can then be used to
break up an entire rock surface. Buzea's experiments have shown that it is
possible to collect up 50 kg of rock in 30 minutes by this method (Buzea 2018)
(Figure 5B). This figure does not, of course, take account of the work involved in
preparing the wooden trough and associated channelling to bring water to the site;

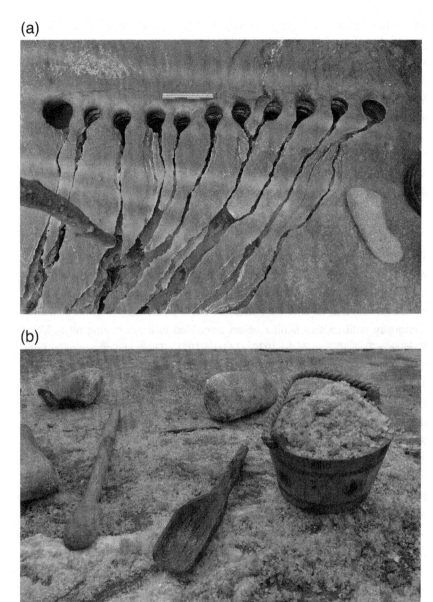

Figure 5 A. Depressions in rock salt produced by letting fresh water drip onto the rock surface. B. Implements used in the reconstruction of salt production by Dan Buzea.

Photos: Dan Buzea/Valeriu Cavruc.

but it is nevertheless an impressive total, for relatively little effort in the gathering process. It is interesting though that this technique is so far only known from a relatively limited area, central and northern Transylvania and the Maramureş (including the adjacent part of Ukraine, formerly known as the northern Maramureş). It would not be surprising to find it in neighbouring Moldavia, or indeed in south-east Poland, but so far this has not happened.

It is not known what happened to the chunks of rock salt that could have been recovered in this way, but in the absence of any evidence that they were ground down to produce usable salt, it is probable that, just as at Hallstatt, the rock was dissolved in pools and evaporated to produce crystals in a purer form.

The Trough Technique

The use of large wooden troughs, supplied by channelled wooden poles bringing water to them, has been shown by recent work to have been a particularly important technique for salt production in one particular part of Europe. This was first noted in what is today Ukraine in the nineteenth century (Preisig 1877), but remained a curiosity until another similar object turned up in a salt-mining pit at Valea Florilor in Transylvania in the 1930s (Maxim 1971). These and other similar finds were finally recognised for what they were when fieldwork in northern Transylvania at the site of Băile Figa near Beclean began in 2005 (Harding & Kavruk 2013). Since then a whole series of troughs has been discovered at Figa (Figure 6): seven at the time of writing, and more from other sites in the area. They were clearly part of an established method of producing salt in the area of present-day Romania, along with the Ukrainian find north of the river Tisza.[2]

All the finds come from salt extraction pits and mines or salty streams. At Figa, the only site to have been scientifically excavated, the troughs lie in or beside the stream bed, close to the rock salt which lies a short distance below. In one area of the site, a series of other installations were found, notably a tapering well-like feature constructed of wattle with a narrow and deep ditch dug in the rock salt through the middle of its base, a straight fence made of upright planks, split troughs, channelled pieces and shovels stuck in the mud down to the rock salt; a roundish wattle fence enclosing the well; a corridor made of two parallel lines of massive poles; a sort of floor made of massive timbers and lying on the rock salt around the well base; as well as five complete troughs and numerous implements of wood and stone (Figure 7). In other areas there are wattle fences forming oval or round constructions, presumed to be for storing concentrated brine, and many other installations of uncertain purpose.

---

[2] Adjacent areas of south-east Poland and western Ukraine might also have utilised this technique, but in the absence of detailed fieldwork this remains speculative.

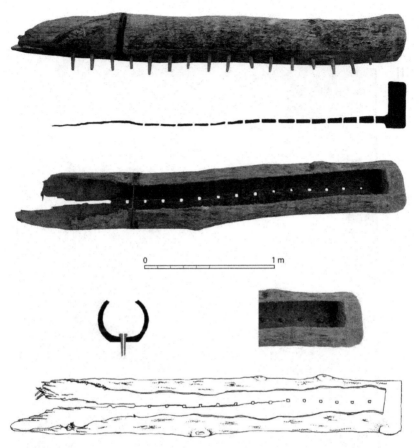

Figure 6 One of the troughs found in excavation at Băile Figa, Beclean, Romania.

Photo: Valeriu Cavruc.

The troughs are hollowed out tree trunks, around 2–3 m long, with a row of perforations in the base. In the best preserved cases, the perforations are filled with pegs, which are themselves perforated, with either twisted cord or long needle-like sticks pushed into the perforation. Accompanying the troughs are other wooden objects, notably channelled pieces and in some cases ladders. The process by which the troughs worked is discussed previously, as is the question of whether the resulting salt was ground down and used as it was, or dissolved and evaporated.

Evaporation

By contrast, the natural distribution of salt across Europe and the presence of springs and streams with a high salt content means that evaporating salt water

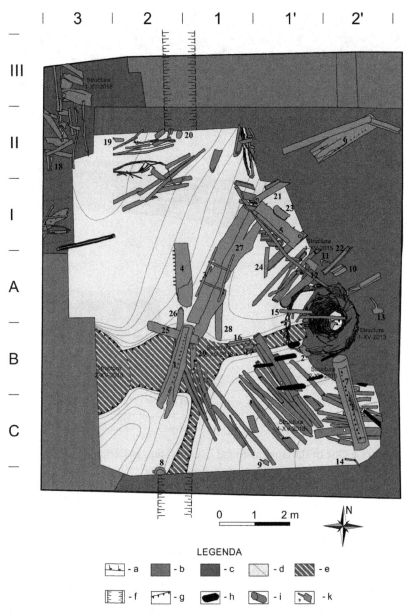

Figure 7 Plan of an area at Băile Figa, near Beclean, Romania, where a series of troughs, fences, and a well-like feature were found. Plan: National Museum of the Eastern Carpathians,

courtesy of Valeriu Cavruc.

was possible in many places and in many different ways. The same applies to seawater. This latter is in many ways less favourable and more laborious because it contains many other minerals and impurities than merely sodium and chlorine ions. Consequently it involves farming the salt in pans, evaporating it for a greater or lesser time, and purifying it to remove the minerals which would impair taste. The brine from salt springs likewise may vary greatly in salinity and often contain salts other than sodium chloride, particularly those regarded as important for their curative properties.

Technically speaking, brine 'designates a solution of salt (usually sodium chloride) in water. In a different context, brine may refer to salt solutions ranging from about 3.5% (a typical concentration of seawater, or the lower end of solutions used for brining foods) up to about 26% (a typical saturated solution, depending on temperature)' (Abdel-Aal *et al.* 2017). These factors apply to salt production in all periods and all areas. The process of concentrating the brine and removing impurities is something that affects all methods of evaporation and all types of brine. Sometimes and with some techniques this is called 'graduation' (i.e. using a series of step changes to increase the concentration). Different kinds of graduation construction have been used historically.

In principle, all that is needed is the application of heat to evaporate the liquid, leaving the salt as crystals on the water surface or adhering to adjacent solid surfaces. The simplest way to do this is through insolation (the natural application of the heat of the sun, or more generally the heat of the atmosphere in the summer months). This is what happens at the numerous salt lagoons around the Mediterranean or on the salt pans where seawater is allowed to flow into fenced areas, often with solid floors which enable the resulting crystals to be collected more easily (around the Mediterranean there are some 90 active sites, out of 170 known historically: Gauci *et al.* 2017). The most extreme cases are salt lakes such as the Tuz Gölü of Turkey, where salt crystals can be picked up around the margins with no additional technology of any sort. Coastal lagoons involve the same processes, except that seawater is not as pure and must be processed further. Salt pans involve more work to produce an acceptable product, for the reasons outlined in the next section. But it is clear from the classical authors that these were the techniques used around Italian shores in historic and probably also in prehistoric times. The same is probably true for other Mediterranean lands, where salt pans are a frequent occurrence at the present day, said to be producing some 7 million tonnes annually (Walmsley 2000).

Evaporating Seawater

Seawater consists of some 96.5 per cent water, 2.5 per cent salts of various kinds, and the rest dissolved inorganic and organic materials and particulates.

The salts consist principally of ions of chlorine, sodium, sulphur, magnesium, calcium and potassium, the precise amounts depending on local and atmospheric conditions. Evaporation of the water – either by heating the water artificially or through insolation – is the first step in the production process. This, however, does not in itself remove the other salts that are undesirable from the point of view of taste, and which can make unprocessed sea salt bitter, hence the term 'bittern' for the product of simple evaporation. For this reason, salt pans typically use a set of techniques to progressively remove the undesirable salts, so that in the later stages sodium chloride precipitates and can be collected by hand or through shovelling.

> When seawater is evaporated soluble salts will be formed, at different stages during the evaporation. The crystallization of the salts dissolved in seawater is governed by their solubility products and occurs at different concentration levels. When seawater is concentrated gradually, brine concentration increases leading to the successive precipitation of the least soluble salts first. For example, iron oxide and calcium carbonate start to crystallize first, in very small quantities, followed by calcium sulfate (known as gypsum) . . . Right at this stage, sodium chloride starts to crystallize out, yielding about 75% of the available sodium chloride (known as halide) in solution. Reaching this stage would correspond to the evaporation of about 97% of the total water. Next, magnesium chloride will start to crystallize as a solid solution along with sodium chloride forming what is called 'bitterns' . . . [These are] a concentrated form of a collection of magnesium, potassium, sulfate and chloride salts, such as KCl [potassium chloride], $MgCl_2$ [magnesium chloride] and $MgSO_4$ [magnesium sulfate] and double salts. (Abdel-Aal *et al.* 2017)

An account of how seawater is turned into usable sodium chloride, based on the processes used in modern saltworks (Cádiz), has been provided by Brais Currás; the progressive stages of evaporation largely correspond to those just described. At Aveiro near Porto in northern Portugal, three stages are utilised: accumulation ponds, concentration zones and crystallisation ponds. The problem of getting rid of the bitterns is a perennial one: he points out:

> in modern saltworks concentration never passes above 30° Bé[3] in order to prevent the co-precipitation of magnesium sulfate and magnesium chloride and its incorporation into the final salt. For this, salt should be harvested directly from the wet brine, before evaporation is complete leaving a hard crust. (Currás 2017)

Currás has used these factors in presenting the Roman salt pans of Galicia in north-western Spain. A similar set of procedures has been described for the

---

[3] The Baumé scale (often written Bé) is used to measure the density of liquids, with distilled water having a value of 0.

Salinas of Poza de la Sal, Burgos (Mangas & del Rosario Hernando 2011: 38–9).

In principle, salt can be produced from seawater anywhere. In a European context, it is around Mediterranean shores that most salt pans are present, but in archaeological terms the evidence is most abundant on Atlantic and North Sea coasts (France, Britain, the Low Countries). Apart from medieval and modern saltmaking in North Frisia, on the western borders of Germany and Denmark, and on the Danish island of Læsø in the Kattegat, there is no evidence for salt production in Scandinavia (www.visitdenmark.com/denmark/explore/laeso-saltsyderi-gdk647613, last accessed 24 November 2020). Since the Baltic Sea has very low salinity (< 1 per cent), evaporating seawater would be immensely laborious; Scandinavian countries have traditionally imported their salt from continental ports such as Lübeck.

When we come to look at ancient evaporation techniques, two authors include significant information about the production of salt in pans. Neither was concerned to provide a scientific account of the process; the passages are parts of poems, and coincidental to the story in question. Rutilius Namatianus, a Gallo-Roman author who was born in the late fourth century AD, describes the pans at Vada (the port of Volterra) in his poem *De reditu suo* (1.475–84):

> We find time to inspect the salt-pans lying near the mansion: it is on this score that value is set upon the salt marsh, where the sea-water, running down through channels in the land, makes entry, and a little trench floods the many-parted ponds. But after the Dog-star [Sirius] has advanced his blazing fires, when grass turns pale, when all the land is athirst [i.e. summer], then the sea is shut out by the barrier-sluices, so that the parched ground may solidify the imprisoned waters. The natural incrustations catch the penetrating sun, and in the summer heat the heavy crust of salt cakes, just as when the wild Danube stiffens with ice and carries huge wains upon its frost-bound stream. Let him who is given to weigh natural causes examine and investigate the different effect worked in the same material: frost-bound streams melt on catching the sun, and on the other hand liquid waters can be hardened in the sun. (translated by J. Wight Duff, Arnold M. Duff. Loeb Classical Library 434. Cambridge, MA: Harvard University Press, 1934)

Marcus Manilius, writing in the early decades of the first century AD, has specific information about the way the pans were used (*Astronomica* 5, 682–92):

> Moreover, such men will be able to fill great salt-pans, to evaporate the sea, and to extract the sea's venom: they prepare a wide expanse of hardened ground and surround it with firm walls, next conduct therein waters channelled from the nearby sea and then deny them exit by closing sluice-gates: so

the floor holds in the waves and begins to glisten as the water is drained off by the sun. When the sea's dry element has collected, Ocean's white locks are shorn for use at table, and huge mounds are made of the solid foam; and the poison of the deep, which prevents the use of sea-water, vitiating it with a bitter taste, they commute to life-giving salt and render a source of health. (Loeb translation, G. P. Goold. Loeb Classical Library 469. Cambridge, MA: Harvard University Press, 1977)

Both these accounts give indications of the process of creating enclosed spaces where seawater was collected for evaporation. Manilius indicates that it was important to get rid of the elements that made salt bitter, as described previously, though he does not specifically say how this was done. For this, information from modern saltworks is valuable, as Currás indicates.

Bill Thayer, a visitor to the salt works at Cervia, near Cesenatico on the Adriatic coast of northern Italy (Figure 8), described his encounter with the workers at the site:

The 835 hectares are cordoned off from the rest of the area by a perimeter canal some 14 km long, which among other more obvious functions serves as a barrier against fresh water: and within that, the whole surface, now a single unit of 9 lagoons but formerly 150 separate family-worked holdings, is a carefully designed course of water channelled and force-pumped into pans of greater and greater salinity, the raw salt water coming in via the

Figure 8 The salt pans at Cervia, near Cesenatico, Italy.

canal at Milano Marittima at 3° Baumé and the salt precipitating at 27° Baumé, then mechanically harvested, packed ... and sold as a specialty salt ... Because Cervia is so far N, the precipitation occurs slowly and can thus be controlled so that only the first fraction of mineral chlorides precipitates, which by good fortune is the sodium; since it's the oligominerals (magnesium, potassium, etc.) that give the sharper taste to sea salt, Cervia's salt is 'sweet.' (penelope.uchicago.edu/Thayer/E/Biographical/Diary/edited/0304/27.html, last accessed 16 September 2020)

One may compare the technology used on the Atlantic coast of France to produce *fleur du sel*, and the terminology specific to these saltworks (www.tradysel.com/en/the-salt-marshes/the-salt-worker-s-profession.html, last accessed 5 November 2020).

Evaporating Brine

Insolation, however, is often insufficient to produce salt quickly enough or in sufficient quantity to supply even local needs if the sun is not strong enough or the atmosphere insufficiently warm – as is often the case in north-western, central or northern Europe. In such cases, heat must be applied through artificial means, in other words, the use of fire. A range of such techniques were adopted in prehistory and early history. Principal among these was the use of fired clay structures and containers which are known by the French term briquetage, that is, brick-like material, in other words, coarse fired clay. This was first noted long ago in the Seille valley in Lorraine, where huge quantities of this material have continued to turn up since. Nowadays the term is often applied just to the containers that were used to hold the brine, but in fact it refers to the whole structure involved – walls, bars and other elements – where fire was lit underneath and the evaporation vessels placed above.

Furnaces using briquetage typically produce archaeological remains that consist of a hearth or pit, containing fragments of the walls of the structure, often the bars onto which the evaporation vessels were placed, the pedestals to support the superstructure, and the vessels themselves, usually fragmentary (Figure 9). These elements are typically pink or whitish in colour, given the effects of the fire and the presence of the salt. The clay used is coarse and full of inclusions; it was never intended for use beyond the industrial process. In this context, one may note that in a number of cases it is claimed that 'ordinary' ceramics were used in the evaporation process (i.e. vessels that are similar to or the same as those used for other everyday purposes). This is a matter of some debate, since one would expect clear signs of the firing process on vessels that originally contained salt. It is easy to try this out at home with a standard cooking range: a clay container filled with brine and

Figure 9 Briquetage from sites in Sachsen-Anhalt.
Source: Ettel, Ipach and Schneider 2018, courtesy of Professor Peter Ettel.

placed on or in such an oven will change colour, and the salt will typically adhere to the vessel walls and base. This is not observed on such standard ceramics that are said to have been used for salt production; clearly the matter requires more experimentation.

In general, however, the vessels involved consisted of conical beakers and trays, in which the brine would be put. Pedestals were frequent at some periods and in some places, but much of the structural material is generally formless.

Using briquetage was evidently very successful in salt production as its application became widespread through western and central Europe in later prehistory, and continued to be used into the Roman and medieval periods. Some areas, however, never adopted it, or if they did, they did not continue with its use. Many places in Germany, France and Britain have produced briquetage, for instance the so-called 'Red Hills' on the east coast of England (which are actually mounds full of burnt material including quantities of briquetage).

Graduation towers can also be used to help with the concentration process. These are wall-like constructions made of thorny bushes, with the brine introduced to run down the wall, the increased surface area enabling evaporation to take place more quickly. Although such constructions are only appropriate today for artisanal salt production, examples can still be seen at a number of places in Germany and Poland.

Other Techniques

Apart from the mining and quarrying of rock salt, and the evaporation of brine, the other techniques that are likely to have been used are those that are attested ethnographically or described by the ancient authors. Principal among these is the use of fire applied to vegetable matter. 'In the provinces of Gaul and Germany they pour salt water on burning logs' (Pliny the Elder, *Natural History* Book 31); 'There is a place [in Umbria] there where reeds and rushes grow: these they burn and throw their ashes into water and boil it till there is only a little left, and this when allowed to cool produces quite a quantity of salt' (Aristotle, *Meteorologica* II.3).

These descriptions show a striking similarity to modern ethnographic accounts. Work in New Guinea has shown how particular plants are soaked in brine and then burned, the salt crystals being picked from the ash and compressed into packets or cakes wrapped in plant material (Pétrequin *et al.* 2000; 2001). It is certainly possible to throw brine onto a fire and collect the salt crystals, though some further processing is needed to purify the resulting salt. A variant is the use of salty mud or sand which can be filtered, through a basketry device, plant ash, or devices involving clay vessels (Liot 2002). Such techniques are known from Mesoamerica and from some parts of Africa; these are the procedures thought to have been used in parts of Atlantic France (Rouzeau 2002).

Most of these methods would leave little or no trace archaeologically. It is reasonable, however, to presume that they would have been used in ancient times, since they are in common use in pre-industrial societies at the present day or the recent past.

A traditional technique which draws on several of these elements has been described by Saitas and Zarkia (2006). This concerns the Mani peninsula of the southern Peloponnese, where the western coast has numbers of small-scale production sites, in use for many years up to modern times. Much is done through the use of natural rock pools, or with some digging into the rock to produce crystallisation ponds higher up the shore where the crystallised salt could be collected; less frequently by the creation of artificial evaporation tanks. The process of producing salt is quite complex, going through six stages and producing different qualities of salt in each stage; but it relates to a basic and no doubt ancient and widespread set of techniques that might occur in almost any part of the Mediterranean.

Relative Efficiency of Different Methods

Clearly, ancient people will have used whichever method of production seemed best, whether through efficiency of production (personpower, quantities produced, ease of obtaining raw materials, connection to transport links), availability of materials, or through conformity to cultural norms in the society in question. It is worth considering which method might have been most efficient in our modern economising terms (which was not necessarily what was most important to ancient people). It is very difficult to specify quantities of salt produced by the different methods, in absolute terms, in relation to the number of people involved, and to the ease with which the salt might have been distributed to consumers. On the face of it, one might suppose that mining operations like those at Hallstatt would have won hands down in terms of output, and certainly the volumes produced over the centuries in which the mines were in use must have amounted to many tonnes. The time period is also considerable, which makes the annual output somewhat less remarkable. Compared to a small-scale briquetage operation, one can argue that there was no comparison between the two. But some briquetage sites are very large indeed, most notably the late Iron Age sites in Lorraine, where tonnes of debris are present, resulting from exploitation over many decades: in the Upper Seille valley these have been estimated at 3 million m^3 (Olivier 2015: 69).

Estimating the quantities obtained from the trough technique is possibly easier, as described previously. But to acquire this salt, there was a great deal of preparatory work involved, in obtaining and preparing the wood, making the troughs, and setting up the water channels. This technique was also in use for several centuries, so what might be produced with one trough on one location does not necessarily mean a large output at any one period.

At the end of the day, one may assume that people produced as much salt as their needs dictated, whether for domestic use or for distribution to a wider constituency. The location and number of such 'consumers' will have varied over time. Since at present it is not possible to tie sources to the end destinations of traded salt, identifying the precise nature of the movement of salt must remain speculative.

3 Production from Earliest Times Down to the Neolithic

We have seen how salt is a biological necessity for humans and animals, and how it has many uses for health and food preservation. It is of interest, therefore, to consider how early one can discern signs that people were specifically seeking out salt. In theory this could go back almost as far as humanity itself, but in practice we know too little about human ancestors before modern humans became established in Europe, at some time during the Palaeolithic (at the time of writing, this seems to lie around 60,000 years BP). In fact there is no specific evidence pointing to Palaeolithic exploitation of salt sources; if it happened, one assumes it took the form of exploiting salt springs or outcropping rock. The proximity of sites to salt sources might be indicative, though hardly conclusive. Meat-eating itself ensures a certain level of salt intake, since the tissues and blood of animals are naturally rich in sodium; animals, especially herbivores, deprived of salt seek it out in salty water or vegetation. It is likely, therefore, that lack of salt was the least of the health worries with which Palaeolithic people had to concern themselves.

The earliest evidence that suggests a specific exploitation of salt sources comes from the Mesolithic, in the form of a salt well at Moriez (Alpes de Haute Provence) in southern France, which produced pieces of pine, one of them worked, that are interpreted as having formed a small enclosure for brine evaporation. Two of these gave radiocarbon dates that fall in the sixth millennium cal BC, the later Mesolithic of the area (Morin 2002; Morin *et al.* 2006). This material is suggestive, while falling short of being conclusive. It is certainly likely that such a brine source would have been known and exploited.

It is with the Neolithic that the evidence for exploitation becomes truly convincing. Recent reviews of the Neolithic evidence have concentrated on the few sites where there is direct evidence for salt production, the proximity of sites to salt sources, and the presence of stone tools that may have been used in the production process (Bánffy 2015; Weller 2015). A site at Lunca-Poiana Slatinei (Tîrgu Neamţ, Moldavia, eastern Romania), where a small tell lying immediately next to a salt well has produced Criş culture pottery, has been described as the earliest salt production site in the world (Weller & Dumitroaia 2005; Weller *et al.* 2008; 2009) (Figure 10). The radiocarbon dates published lie in the earlier sixth millennium cal BC. Indeed, given the closeness of the site to the well, it would be astonishing if there was not a direct connection between the two. A full publication of these important discoveries is awaited.

Other evidence from Romania has been known for many years. As long ago as 1977, Nicolae Ursulescu published ceramics from a site at Solca-Slatina Mare in Suceava county which looked very much like briquetage (Ursulescu 1977); such material can still be seen at the site today. At Cacica in the same county similar material has been found, accompanied by rather later (Cucuteni) pottery (Andronic 1989); here, at various points around the (now disused) salt mine such briquetage is frequent (Figure 11). There are, however, no spots at which the brine boiling process can be shown to have occurred. Pottery plausibly interpreted as briquetage has been identified at a series of other Neolithic (Cucuteni) sites in Moldavia (Diaconu 2018). One of those that has been excavated is Ţolici-Hălăbutoaia in Neamţ district (Dumitroaia *et al.* 2008).

Somewhat later, a remarkable site in eastern Bulgaria at Provadia, inland from Varna, has been the subject of detailed examination in recent years by Vassil Nikolov (Nikolov 2008; 2009). Here a tell belonging to the Neolithic and

Figure 10 The tell site of Poiana Slatinei, Lunca (near Târgu-Neamț, Romania). The salt well lies at its foot, now enclosed in a hollowed-out tree-trunk.

Photo: author.

Figure 11 Briquetage from Cacica, Suceava county, Romania.

Photo: author.

Chalcolithic lies over a salt diapir and beside a modern salt mine. Large quantities of thin-walled bowls were recovered from a building containing an oven, the assumption being that the bowls were used for evaporating brine (Weller 2012). This process went on for many centuries, leading to the recovery of great numbers of ceramics.

It was in the subsequent Middle Chalcolithic period, assigned to 4700–4200 cal BC, and thus contemporary at least in part with the famous cemetery at nearby Varna, that the major development of salt production at Provadia took place. This area, partly overlying installations of the preceding phase, covered more than 0.5 ha and contained at least five large salt-making installations. These were again large pits, filled with very large quantities of sherd material (Figure 12). Large open tub or bucket-like vessels, with rusticated surface and flat base, in three sizes, are typical (Weller 2012: 71–3, figs. 5–6). These were apparently packed into the bottom of the pits, wood added and lit, and the whole thing allowed to boil and then cool, so that brine was turned into crystals in conical cake form; the pot would then be smashed and the cake retrieved. The quantities of salt produced were evidently very large; the vessels

Figure 12 Part of the large quantity of broken sherds, interpreted as salt-boiling vessels, from Provadia-Solnitsata, Bulgaria.

Photo: author.

could contain between 1 and 80 litres of brine, theoretically producing some-where between 1.1 and 170 kg of salt in cake form (Weller 2012: 80–1, figure 16).

Elsewhere in the Balkans, Neolithic salt production is claimed for the Tuzla area in Bosnia, also an area of modern salt mining. The evidence here consists of ceramics of the Vinča period claimed to be briquetage (Benac 1978), while the proximity of earlier sites to salt sources has also been regarded as suggestive (Tasić 2000). Similar suggestions have been made for Transylvania (Lazarovici & Lazarovici 2011).

The other area where Late Neolithic and Chalcolithic exploitation is evi-denced is southern Poland. Small conical vessels have long been known from the area around the great salt mines of Bochnia and Wieliczka, and can be seen in the Wieliczka Saltworks Museum in Little Poland (Jodłowski 1971; 1977; Fraś 2001). These come from Lengyel period sites, notably at Barycz south of Kraków, where site VII is usually cited (Grabowska 1967; Jodłowski 1968; 1971: 111, figure 24; Bukowski 1985: 46–7, figure 8). Here a series of slight ditches was present, two of them apparently leading into roughly square pits with sides of 2 m or 1.8 m (interpreted as settling tanks), with hearths and a large wooden construction also present. Many other sites of the same period are present in the greater Kraków area, which suggests an intense interest in the salt sources, just as happened later on in the Bronze Age.

While I have concentrated here on Europe, one should not ignore the situation in Turkey, where, as well as a number of rock salt sites, there is the Great Salt Lake (Tuz Gölü) to consider. As far as I am aware, there is no definite evidence linking it with the great settlements of the Neolithic in central Anatolia, most famously Çatal Höyük; but it would be surprising if the salt from the lake was not widely distributed. It is also worth mentioning the salt mines at Duzdaği in Azerbaijan (Marro *et al.* 2010; Marro 2011); the accounts published so far indicate a date in the second half of the fifth millennium BC (based on the Late Chalcolithic Chaff-Faced Ware present in part of the site: Marro 2010). This work is ongoing; a recent discussion of the stone tools from the site has shed much light on the production methods (Hamon 2016). Interestingly, these show very limited interest in grinding salt, an impression which Caroline Hamon has been kind enough to confirm (*in litt.* 28 August 2016).

In Iberia there is now some evidence for Neolithic salt production. At La Marismilla (La Puebla del Río, Seville) excavation has recovered a series of hearths full of pottery (Escacena Carrasco & Garcia Rivero 2019). Analysis of the stratigraphy and the finds suggest that this is the earliest evidence of salt production in Iberia, dated to the fourth millennium cal BC (Late Neolithic), and therefore one of the earliest salt production sites in western Europe. As at Provadia, salt was heated in large ceramic vessels. Other sites of the fourth millennium BC include Fuente Camacho near Granada (Terán Manrique & Morgado 2011) and Monte da Quinta site 2, Santarém, on the Tagus estuary in Portugal, where extensive excavation revealed burnt structures and 'briquetage bulks' – large quantities of broken pottery interpreted as briquetage (Valera 2017). This pottery consisted largely of small conical thin-walled vessels, which were placed over a pit filled with pebbles, serving as low-temperature heating structures to boil the brine. There were also clay brackets to hold the vessels in place, knapped river pebbles, and larger pots used in the initial firing stage to start the concentration of the brine. When the salt crystals had formed in the small pots, they would be broken to extract the salt cake. The volumes of salt obtained were potentially large – each vessel has a capacity of 32 decilitres, giving a potential total of 1293 litres (1784 kg) from the excavated part of the site. A series of radiocarbon dates from similar sites in the area indicated a time bracket between the middle of the fourth millennium and the early centuries of the third.

In Catalonia, the Salt Mountain (Muntanya de Sal) at Cardona, where there is a modern salt mine (no longer working), is potentially important. While there is no specific site indicating ancient salt production, numerous finds of stone axes have come from the area, some showing signs of grinding and battering (Weller 2002; Figuls *et al.* 2007; Weller & Figuls 2007; Fíguls *et al.* 2013). These tools were mostly of hard rock that is not available locally, suggesting that the use to which they were put was so important that it necessitated movement of stone along trade routes – similar to the movement of variscite (callaïs, turquoise) from the mines of Gavà south-west of Barcelona (Borrell *et al.* 2015; Querré *et al.* 2019).

Lastly, for Spain, there are now suggestions that production at the great salt pans of Añana may have started life in the Neolithic (Martínez Torrecilla *et al.* 2013; Guerra Doce 2016: 97).

In recent years, important new evidence for Neolithic salt production has emerged from both France and Britain. In western France, the site of Champ-Durand at Nieul-sur-l'Autise, a fortified site with multiple rings of fortification similar to British causewayed enclosures, produced a significant amount of coarse pottery that is surely to be connected with salt boiling (Ard & Weller 2012); small conical vessels look very similar to those known from Poland, and the chlorine content was also higher than would be expected. Radiocarbon dates indicate a date in the second half of the fourth millennium BC. Similar pottery is known from a number of other sites in the Vendée and adjacent regions of western France, associated mainly with late Neolithic enclosures. Suggestions along these lines had been made previously by Serge Cassen (Cassen *et al.* 2008). This puts flesh on the bones of earlier suggestions that there might have been Neolithic salt pans in Brittany, given the extensive evidence for Neolithic activity there (Gouletquer & Weller 2002; Cassen *et al.* 2006). More recently, excavations at Street House, Loftus, North Yorkshire, north-east England, has produced an ovoid pit, with much burning, and a potential brine storage tank, along with coarse ceramics that are certainly briquetage, and radiocarbon dates falling in the middle of the fourth millennium BC (Sherlock 2021). Although Neolithic salt working has been suggested for Britain before (Brothwell & Brothwell 1969: 160–2), this is the first secure finding of salt-working debris. It remains a puzzle as to why this evidence is found on ground some 170 m above the seashore, which, though only a short distance from the sea as the crow flies, requires a much longer journey to the beach.

In summary, it is clear that salt production was under way in the European Neolithic, with circumstantial evidence for efforts in this regard in the preceding Mesolithic. A number of things stand out. First, there was no one way of producing salt in these early periods: while briquetage or pottery substituting for briquetage is present in some places, in others it is more likely that surface quarrying using hammerstones was more likely; and that solar evaporation involving no artificial aids at all was carried out, leaving no archaeological trace. The evidence of proximity between archaeological sites and salt sources is circumstantial, but in view of the universal need for salt it is more than likely that these proximities represent a real association. It is with the next period of prehistory, however, that these matters can be placed on a much more secure footing.

4 The Copper and Bronze Ages

With the Bronze Age, we enter into a new chapter in the history of salt production in Europe. While there are still many uncertainties in the interpretation of the available archaeological evidence, in general it becomes possible to see regularised forms of production, with different techniques being used in the different parts of Europe.

It is in this period, too, that we come across the first known finds of actual salt in archaeological contexts. Most spectacular was the discovery of a deposit of half a kilo of salt in broken pottery containers in the Ourania cave in eastern Crete (Kopaka & Chaniotakis 2003). The reasons for the deposition of the material are unclear, but given the nature of the site a ritual purpose may be likely – something that would support the idea of a special importance being assigned to salt. The only other secure finding is that from a pit on a Bronze Age site in western Hungary (Németh 2013) (Figure 13). The excavator connected

Figure 13 Piece of rock salt found in excavation in a pit at Lébény-Kaszásdomb, Győr-Moson-Sopron county, Hungary.

Photo: courtesy of Gabriella Németh.

this find with the issue of salt distribution in the Late Bronze Age. Given the solubility of salt, it is hardly surprising that it rarely survives archaeologically; these finds can be regarded as the result of a lucky chance – especially the Hungarian example, given the conditions expected in such a pit.

The salt from the Ourania cave were presumably produced by solar evaporation from coastal salt lagoons; the Hungarian find could have come from the mines of the eastern Alps, though since it is not possible to identify from which source salt comes, this remains speculative.

If these finds are exceptional, what we can expect by way of evidence for salt production usually comes in the form of the remains of artefacts or installations utilised in the process. The exception to this is mining for rock salt, most notably at Hallstatt, but probably also in other areas where rock salt outcrops at or near the earth's surface. Mining need not always go deep into the ground: in some cases, as we shall see, it consists of open-cast working, which is in essence quarrying.

As with other periods, these finds are usually fragmentary and almost always hard to understand in detail. For the most part, we are talking about briquetage, mainly containers for brine evaporation rather than the furnace installations. In coastal areas, particularly in the Mediterranean (above all around Italian shores), there is evidence for the exploitation of sea water through evaporation in specialised containers. The other technique which occurs, and only in one area of Europe, is the so-called trough technique, found in Transylvania.

Mining and Quarrying

Discussion of salt mining in the Bronze Age inevitably starts from the well-known mines at Hallstatt in the Salzkammergut of central Austria. The subject of intense interest and activity since the middle of the nineteenth century, Hallstatt was initially known for its prehistoric cemetery, mainly though not exclusively of Early Iron Age date. It was quickly realised that the existence of this cemetery might be connected with the salt mine that was the main economic resource of the area, with a known history stretching as far back as the available records went. This connection has been maintained since, and remains a plausible motive for the construction of a rich cemetery 300 m up on a plateau above the eponymous lake; salt working was active then as it is now, though naturally the technology has completely changed over the centuries. The ancient mine shafts are filled with a mass of deposits known to the miners of modern times as *Heidengebirge* ('heathens' rock'), a mass of mining waste full of a great variety of artefacts and ecofacts (Kern *et al.* 2009: 36–9).

Although the initial exploration of ancient shafts suggested it belonged solely to the Iron Age, by the middle of the twentieth century it had become clear that some of the workings were older and fell in the Bronze Age. The mining areas at Hallstatt are divided into groups of shafts, each shaft given its own name. It was in the Northern Group of shafts that the Bronze Age material came to light, particularly in the Appoldwerk, Grünerwerk and Christian von Tuschwerk (Kern *et al.* 2009: 50ff.). The first radiocarbon dates from these areas showed that they fell in the Bronze Age (Barth *et al.* 1975); more recent dendrochono-logical work has confirmed that a large number of workings and artefacts in wood belong to the Middle and Late Bronze Age (Grabner *et al.* 2006; Grabner *et al.* 2007). The quantity and quality of the preserved finds in the shafts is extraordinary. Large amounts of timbering allowed the miners to penetrate deep into the mountain, even though the sides of the shafts were not timbered. Well-preserved ropes made from lime bast run along the shafts, presumably for hauling the extracted lumps of rock out; large numbers of tapers indicate lighting methods. Two truly remarkable finds must be mentioned: a well-constructed wooden staircase, dated dendrochronologically to 1344–1343 BC (Grabner *et al.* 2007; Kern *et al.* 2009: 61–3), which enabled the miners to move across heaps of mining spoil from one level to another; and a knapsack made of untanned cow skin, capable of carrying up to 30 kg of rock salt (Kern *et al.* 2009: 60–1) (Figure 14).

As well as such finds in wood and other organic materials, a number of bronze picks have been found at Hallstatt and elsewhere (Mayer 1977: 228–9, Taf. 92–3). These were used to create parallel vertical grooves on the rock surface,

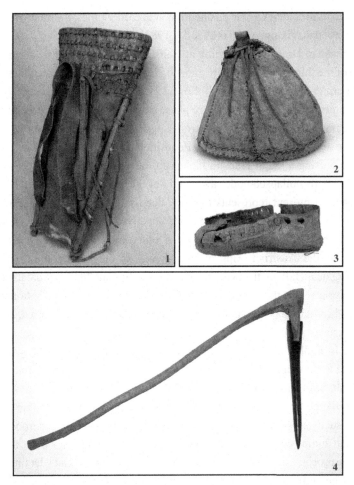

Figure 14 Implements of Bronze Age date found in the Hallstatt mine.
Photos: A. Rausch, courtesy of NHM Vienna.

after which the material between the grooves was hammered out in chunks for transport to the surface.

Work in the mines must have been cramped, hot and smelly, not to say dangerous. The shafts are typically only wide enough for a single person to pass through, except in those areas where a significant amount of rock had been extracted – and before it then filled up again with spoil from new workings. Some idea of the working conditions can be deduced from the fact that the fill of the shafts contains not only large numbers of tapers for light, but also copious quantities of excrement. For us such a scenario seems strange; but it must indicate that the miners spent considerable amounts of time underground, presumably eating there as well as defecating. *Autres temps, autres mœurs*;

such a situation cannot have been uncommon in earlier times; a similar situation was observed at Viking-Age York (Jones 1983).[4]

The phase of Bronze Age mining at Hallstatt came to an end by around the middle of the thirteenth century BC; no wooden object has been dated later than 1245 (Kern *et al.* 2009: 66), to be followed by an apparent gap in activity until the ninth century, when the Iron Age phase began. Why mining ceased at this point is unclear, but the Hallstatt team suggests that heavy rainfall caused excessive water to enter the shafts, depositing a large amount of sediment, and also causing a major landslip higher up the slope, with the result that the adits and shafts collapsed under the weight of the material washed in.

Hallstatt at present represents the only deep salt mine definitely known to have been exploited in the Bronze Age, but given the existence of suitable mining technology it would be strange if other sites were not also worked, whether in the Austrian Alps or elsewhere. At the nearby mines of the Dürrnberg near Hallein, the evidence indicates only a late Iron Age date, though it is always possible that earlier finds will one day turn up. I have mentioned the outcrops in Muntenia (Romania) which could surely have been worked, at least on the surface.

There is another aspect of the salt mining at Hallstatt: it is not known what happened to the chunks of salt rock. In theory, they could have been ground into edible salt, but there are no grinding tools from the site which could have been used for the purpose (pers. comm. Kerstin Kowarik). It is possible that quern-stones, usually supposed to be for grain-grinding, were used for the purpose. The rough salt lumps could have been transported and ground elsewhere; alternatively, the process could have been what happened in medieval and later times, the salt rock being placed in water and dissolved, the resulting brine then boiled to produce crystalline salt. At present this is a problem that remains unresolved. The situation with the salt from Băile Figa is much the same.

Salt Boiling: Briquetage and Other Techniques in the Copper and Bronze Ages

Important and impressive though the operations at Hallstatt are, in fact the technology was not that utilised in most parts of Europe during the Bronze Age.

---

[4] One may compare the fact that at the present day teenage boys working in coltan (columbite-tantalite) mines in the Democratic Republic of Congo work underground from dawn till dusk, and since the managers do not want the miners to stop work, traders take food down to them. Coltan is mined in order to extract the tantalum, a hardening metal used mainly to make electrolytic capacitors found in mobile phones and other electronic devices, with some uses in the arms industry. The overwhelming need of the world for such minerals has cemented its status as a 'conflict resource', the need making the consumer and the manufacturer unconcerned about its origin or the conditions of its production. Was salt similarly so important to ancient society?

Much the most common was salt evaporation, either by boiling using ceramic containers placed in or on a fire or – where the strength of the sun was great enough – by allowing salt water to dry in lagoons or pans. Archaeologically speaking, the former is much easier to spot than the latter, since it leaves pieces of coarse pottery (briquetage). The latter must, however, have been the normal process along Mediterranean shores.

Briquetage of Bronze Age date (*sensu* coarse pottery, usually with signs of the effects of fire) is known from many parts of central and western Europe: Germany, Poland, France, Spain, Britain and elsewhere. Pride of place goes to the area around Halle (Saale) in Sachsen-Anhalt, east-central Germany, where numerous places have produced sherds or even complete vessels of this ceramic. Known since the nineteenth century, the work of Karl Riehm and Waldemar Matthias in the 1950s, 60s and 70s set the study of the material on a scientific footing (Riehm 1954; 1960; 1962; Matthias 1961; 1976). Matthias in particular produced a vessel typology which accounts for the majority of the Bronze Age vessels recovered. These include a range of forms: trays in which the brine was placed over the fire, pedestals to support the trays, conical beakers and similar forms to contain the damp crystals as they formed. Most of this material belongs to the Early Bronze Age, but briquetage is present in Late Bronze Age contexts too, also in Saxony and Brandenburg, and interestingly in graves as well as settlements (Bönisch 1993; Jockenhövel 2012). The area around Halle in particular saw a significant industry based on salt production, and while the output of a single site may not have been very large, taking them all together the volumes involved must have been substantial.

The material from Brehna, deriving from rescue excavations in 2003–4, adds significantly to the situation (von Rauchhaupt & Schunke 2010). From the Early Bronze Age, a pottery kiln contained a number of oval trays that are argued to be briquetage; a number of burials in settlements in the area also contain briquetage. A great deal more came from Late Bronze and Early Iron Age features, considered in Section 5.

Of the many other localities in Germany where salt production took place – such as Bad Reichenhall in Bavaria, Bad Nauheim in Hesse or Lüneburg in Lower Saxony – while there is abundant evidence for later working, there is no definite evidence for working in the Bronze Age. Since new finds are being made all the time, notably with rescue excavation in advance of development in town centres, this situation could easily change.

In Poland, abundant briquetage has been found on Lausitz culture sites near Kraków, notably Bieżanów site 27 and Rżąka site 1 (Kadrow 2003; Kadrow & Nowak-Włodarczak 2003) (Figure 15). The forms here are absolutely typical:

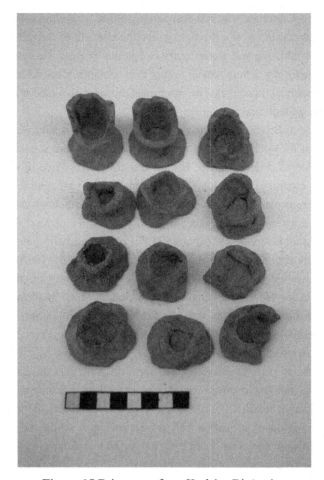

Figure 15 Briquetage from Kraków-Bieżanów.

Photo: author.

most commonly goblets with splaying foot, though not pedestals or trays (perhaps suggesting that the precise form of the furnace was different from those in Early Bronze Age Halle). In other areas, domestic pottery has sometimes been suggested to have served as briquetage, but this remains speculative in the absence of installations that might have served for salt boiling. Many other parts of Poland have salt sources, but at present little or nothing is known of ancient exploitation, in the form of briquetage, on them. An exception is the extreme south-eastern part of the country, where possible briquetage of Bronze Age date has been found near Tyrawa Solna (Dębiec *et al.* 2015; Dębiec & Saile 2018).

In France, briquetage is known from a number of Bronze Age sites, as recently discussed by Cyril Marcigny (Marcigny *et al.* 2020). One example comes from a double enclosure at Étaples-Mont Bagarre, in the Canche valley (Pas-de-Calais), associated with Middle Bronze Age pottery, though without any ovens (Desfossés 2000; Marcigny & Le Goaziou 2012); another from Fermanville (Manche) at the north of the Cotentin peninsula (Marcigny *et al.* 2020: 94–5, figure 3). In many other areas where there is abundant evidence for Iron Age salt production, there is a Bronze Age presence without specific indications of production, for instance in Brittany (Giot *et al.* 1965; Gouletquer 1969; 1970). While no briquetage as such was recovered from the site, excavations at Salies-du-Salat (Haute Garonne) in south-west France produced a range of features, including four vats formed by water-tight clay-lined pits, a hearth, an arrangement of large numbers of Middle Bronze Age sherds from big pottery vessels that may have formed a kind of container, and a pit filled with blocks of ophite with more sherds (Marcigny & Le Goaziou 2012).

In Britain, the number of sites now known to have produced Bronze Age briquetage has increased enormously in recent years. While the majority are in the east of England, especially in Lincolnshire and East Anglia, finds are now known from many other areas (expertly catalogued by Janice Kinory: 2012). Some of these sites may represent the transport rather than the production of salt; it is possible that the evaporated brine, in crystalline form in the ceramic containers, was moved whole and broken up at its destination.

A particularly important site is at Brean Down, Somerset, on the Bristol Channel. The briquetage is associated with Middle Bronze Age contexts (J. Foster in Bell 1990: 165ff.). The finds were made at the foot of a steep cliff just above the beach, and consist of a standard range of pedestals and trays (Figure 16). It is likely that other sites along the coast in this region also produced salt, but at present the evidence from the area only includes Roman and medieval sites. It is possible that some have been lost to rising sea levels. Like sites on or near the east coast of England, such as Billingborough (Chowne *et al.* 2001), the exploitation, based on simple briquetage forms, was probably small in scale, quite unlike that from the later Red Hills.

In Spain and Portugal, work in recent years has produced many Copper and Bronze Age sites with briquetage-like pottery (Terán Manrique 2011; Guerra Doce 2016). Spain is rich in salt deposits; as well as coastal sites there are many inland lagoons and lakes where salt is produced. In a number of places near such lagoons, burnt areas occur, associated with Bronze Age pottery and ceramics that could have served for salt boiling. A typical example is the much-discussed site of Espartinas (Ciempozuelos, near Madrid), where areas of burning, probably connected with the evaporation of brine in large coarse pottery vessels, were accompanied by Chalcolithic and Beaker pottery (Valiente Cánovas & Ayanagüena Sanz 2005; Valiente Cánovas & Ramos 2009).

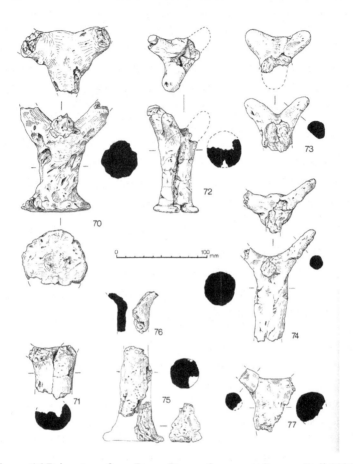

Figure 16 Briquetage from Brean Down, Somerset. Source: Bell 1990,
reproduced courtesy of English Heritage.

The area of Villafáfila in Castilla y León province in central Spain has
been the focus of much fieldwork in recent years (Abarquero Moras &
Guerra Doce 2010; Abarquero Moras *et al.* 2010; Guerra Doce *et al.* 2011;
Abarquero Moras *et al.* 2012), with many sites producing areas of burning
and pottery that appears to have served for brine boiling. Much of this
material is of Chalcolithic and Beaker date, but at Santioste Early and
Middle Bronze Age pottery was present and the site produced much burnt
clay, pits, as well as briquetage and a number of 'combustion structures'
(Abarquero Moras *et al.* 2012: 222ff.). These latter are elongated pits with
clay linings fired pink and red, and much evidence of firing debris.

An intriguing suggestion, recently made by Elisa Guerra Doce (2016; 2017), is that the decoration on Spanish Beaker pottery imitates the basketry and textiles that may have been used for the transport of salt in cake form. The spread of Beakers might thus be in some way associated with trade routes used for other commodities, salt being among them; and control over salt circulation might have been one of the ways in which powerful people came to prominence in the Copper Age.

Coastal Italy has seen a number of investigations into Bronze Age salt production. On the Tyrrhenian side, Isola di Coltano south of Pisa, and the area near Nettuno in southern Lazio, have produced evidence in the form of burnt material associated with large quantities of pottery, and at Isola di Coltano cylindrical or square-sectioned firedogs (probably serving as pedestals in the boiling process) (Di Fraia & Secoli 2002; Pasquinucci & Menchelli 2002; Nijboer *et al.* 2005/2006). One suggestion is that the medium-sized vessels at the site might have been used for solar evaporation, a crust of sodium chloride forming on the top of the brine and easily removed by hand (Di Fraia 2011). On the Adriatic side, there are salt pans at various places along the coast where ancient salt production is likely. At the head of the Adriatic, similar material at Stramare has been found near the mouth of the river Ospo, perhaps where preliminary brine concentration took place, the final processing happening at the castelliere of Elleri, where a considerable quantity of briquetage is present (Cassola Guida & Montagnari Kokelj 2006; Montagnari Kokelj 2007). These authors point out that the salt production activities found at present around the Gulf of Trieste are no doubt very ancient, even if it remains hard to be sure that the surviving evidence indicates Bronze Age production. Further south, on the Dalmatian coast, horn-shaped pillars (pedestals) are present in the museum at Senj, emanating from three Bronze Age sites (Forenbaher 2013).

In sum, across Europe, the standard technique for producing salt in the Bronze Age was evaporation, whether through the heat of the sun or through the use of fire in ovens and furnaces. It is only in a couple of areas that these techniques were not used; they are the exceptions that prove the rule.

The Trough Technique

One of these is the trough technique, described previously. Particularly important is the site of Băile Figa near Beclean in Romania, where no less than seven examples and many fragments have been found (five of them in or near the same trench). So far, all the radiocarbon dates on these objects fall in the Bronze Age, though it is possible that they continued in use beyond that period The quantity of salt that could be produced by this method is impressive, as the figures quoted show. At the same time, there was much hidden labour involved in it, notably with acquiring the necessary timber and fashioning the troughs, to say nothing of the additional work involved in turning the rock salt into usable form (whether by grinding or by dissolving and re-evaporating). It is very likely that the quantities produced were far in excess of local needs; in other words, much of what was produced must have been intended for export to other areas that were not so well supplied.

It is a curious fact that this part of Europe employed this very specific technique for salt production in the Bronze Age (and maybe later as well), while apparently ignoring the briquetage method, which was otherwise the standard technique in inland Europe. One may suppose that once invented, no one would wish to go back to a much less productive method, even if it was simpler to use. That in itself raises the question of why an apparently superior technique did not then travel more widely across the continent. This is not a question that can be answered satisfactorily; it seems that traditions of salt production were strong enough in each area to ensure that the ones initially developed were the ones that continued in use.

5 From Iron Age to Roman in Northern Europe

Salt production in the Iron Age was of a different order of magnitude than that in all preceding periods. This applies not only to the most famous salt production site of all, Hallstatt, but also to the salt marsh and seawater evaporation sites along Atlantic coasts, where very large numbers of sites have been discovered. Because in continental Europe the technology was basically the same in both the pre-Roman Iron Age and the Roman period, it is convenient to treat the two together. For the Mediterranean area, however, I leave the question of production in the Greek and Roman periods to Section 6.

Hallstatt in the Austrian Alps, which we have already met in the context of Bronze Age production, reached its apogee in the Iron Age. This is not to say, however, that it was always the most productive place, or that the techniques adopted there were used widely across Europe: they were not. Most salt elsewhere was produced by evaporating salt water, whether in coastal lagoons and pans through solar evaporation; by leaching and filtering mud or sand from salt marshes; or by boiling brine in clay containers using applied heat. Given the infrequency with which salt outcrops in a way that allows it to be mined or quarried, it is not surprising that the evaporation techniques were by far the most common, in this as in most subsequent periods.

Mining

At Hallstatt, new shafts were opened in the Iron Age, mainly in the East Group of shafts, and most notably in the Kilbwerk (where the 'Man in the salt' was discovered in 1734), the Stügerwerk, and (most recently) the Kernverwässerungswerk ('Core dissolving facility', i.e. where the rock salt was dissolved) (Barth 1990; Rausch 2007; Kern *et al.* 2009: 84–5). This last has been studied since 1990, and a total of nine gallery levels excavated. These were each some 2 m high, one above the other, and all of them full of mining debris. Unlike in the Bronze Age, when shafts were sunk vertically downwards, in the Iron Age adits were cut horizontally to follow the veins of rock salt. The resulting galleries were very large: one that connected the three working areas mentioned is over 170 m long, 5 to 27 m wide and up to 20 m high. It is unknown quite how the miners excavated such an enormous volume, but it is likely they started at the bottom and worked upwards, using a succession of levels to stand on (Stöllner 1999: 36ff.; Kern *et al.* 2009: 84ff.).

Bronze picks continued to be used at Hallstatt, though at the Dürrnberg near Hallein iron was used. A very particular technique was used with the picks: heart-shapes were formed by picking round an area on the rock wall, and blocks in that shape prised off. Such blocks varied greatly in size, presumably depending on the skill of the miner or the nature of the rock at that particular point; while the recovered examples weigh up to 42 kg, negatives on the rock wall suggest that others might have weighed as much as 100 kg – too heavy for one person to lift alone – and also indicating that the blocks were simply carried out of the mine along the adits, not hoisted up shafts with ropes. In addition, the waste material from the chipping out of the blocks was simply left on the ground, not gathered up as they had been in the Bronze Age. This seems a curiously wasteful approach to what was a valuable resource, but presumably the integrity of the blocks was considered more important than spending time gathering up small pieces.

Numerous finds of organic materials have been found in the Iron Age galleries, including leather for shoes and a range of wooden bowls and boxes, presumably from which to eat. Spruce and fir tapers were used to light the work underground; huge numbers of these were also found in excavations at both Hallstatt and the Dürrnberg. Large amounts of organic material survive from the Iron Age levels explored, notably excrement (as in the Bronze Age shafts), which have given unrivalled insights into daily life of the miners. The mining waste (*Heidengebirge*), with its fill of organic and other materials, fills the ancient galleries and shafts. In addition, there is evidence in some places for fires having been lit underground, which might have served to assist in ventilation, though the resulting smoke must have been both hazardous and unpleasant.

Activity in the Early Iron Age, part of the mine came to an end, perhaps suddenly, in the middle of the fourth century BC, when rock falls and inflow of fine sediment filled the galleries and shafts (Kern *et al.* 2009: 156ff.). Activity moved further up the hill, where adits were cut in the Dammwiese in the La Tène period (second century BC). This area has been extensively damaged by historic and modern mining, so little is known about it, but it appears to have been extensive. By this time, however, activity at the Dürrnberg was advanced. The two mining areas together must have produced enormous quantities of rock salt, which was no doubt moved far and wide, north and south of the Alps.

Extensive modern excavations at the Dürrnberg have taken place, with dendrochronology and finds evidence showing exploitation from the fifth century BC onwards; the various mining areas were worked through to the late La Tène period (Stöllner 1999; 2002; 2003). The deep shafts here have again produced huge quantities of organic material. Also here are signs of 'catastrophes', in the form of an influx of sediments in flooding events; a massive event of this kind took place in the second half of the fourth century BC (dendro-dated) (Stöllner 2003: 136–7, figure 10).

Not all rock salt removal can be termed 'mining', but rather 'quarrying', if it involved simply digging out blocks of rock from surface or near-surface deposits. While there are many rock salt outcrops in the Alps and parts of the Carpathians, some of which have surely been exploited, the only one which can demonstrably be shown to have been used is Băile Figa in Romania, discussed previously for its unusual Bronze Age exploitation. In this case, radiocarbon dating demonstrated that certain features (pits and shafts) leading down to the rock surface dated to the Iron Age. It is not known how extensive this phase of exploitation was, or how long it lasted, but the site clearly continued in operation, perhaps after a break, through several centuries of the Iron Age.

Evaporation Techniques

It is during the Iron Age that brine boiling really came into its own. Hundreds of sites, especially in the western countries of Europe, can be shown to have engaged in the practice; typically it is briquetage in various forms that indicates the one-time existence of the practice. Some of the sites involved are small and were probably used only once or for a short time; others are large, and used over and over again for the production of large quantities of crystalline salt. In different areas, the precise pattern of production varied; that is to say, the briquetage involved might be simple or more complex. In relatively few cases is there enough surviving evidence to provide a full and clear picture of exactly how the operations were conducted. Although the precise details of the technology varied between different areas and over time, the general principle was always the same: salty water was available from the sea or salt springs, in some places it was stored in pits, then added to the coarse clay containers and subjected to heating until crystals formed. Briquetage and ovens have been recovered from Iron Age and early Roman contexts in many parts of central and western Europe, especially Britain and France, but also Belgium, Germany, and the Netherlands (Figure 17). Such finds do not occur in Scandinavia, probably because the low salinity of the Baltic makes the process unviable.

The situation with salt production in Roman times in north-western Europe is in many ways a continuation of that in the Iron Age. Many of the Red Hills of eastern England, and of the numerous briquetage sites on the coast of France and Belgium, contain Roman material (Miles 1975; Thoen 1975; Cabal & Thoen 1985; Fawn *et al.* 1990; Lane & Morris 2001; Lane 2018: chap. 6); indeed, in many cases it is impossible to separate the Iron Age from the early Roman sites as salt making continued on them through the first century BC to the first AD, with little or no change in technology.

France

France saw a huge amount of salt production in the Iron Age, with several sites providing very well-preserved evidence for the technology involved. French scholars have written extensively about the topic in recent years, on the basis of highly informative and well-conducted excavations. As a result, much is known about the technological processes involved in salt production in the French Iron Age.

Reviews of the evidence for Iron Age and Roman salt working in north-west Europe, and France in particular, have been presented by Jean-Claude Hocquet (1994; 2001), though much has happened since he wrote. Other authors who have made major contributions to the topic are Laurent Olivier (many articles, referenced in the following pages), Gilles Prilaux (2000), Olivier Weller (many contributions), and Marie-Yvane Daire (2003), as well as earlier authors such as Pierre Louis Gouletquer. A recent survey of the situation on the coastal areas of north-west France is especially useful (Carpentier & Marcigny 2019).

As in many parts of north-west Europe, the evaporation of seawater or brine using briquetage continued unbroken from the late Iron Age into the Early Roman period, with precise chronological division often impossible. Thus some of the basic surveys, such as those by Gouletquer, Daire and others, cover as much early Roman material as they do 'Gallic' (Gaulish) (Daire 2003; Prilaux *et al.* 2011): many are 'Gallo-Roman' in date, which can cover a wide span from the later second century BC to the imperial period.

Of the many sites and areas with important information available, it is necessary above all to discuss those in the Seille valley in Lorraine, the work

(a)

(b)

Figure 17 Briquetage from Brehna, district Anhalt-Bitterfeld, Saxony-Anhalt (von Rauchhaupt & Schunke 2010). A. Column-shaped briquetage from Befund 120; B. 'Trumpet-shaped' briquetage from Befund 1151.

Photos Andrea Hörentrup, courtesy of the Landesamt für Denkmalpflege und Archäologie Sachsen-Anhalt.

along the line of the A16 motorway in the Pas-de-Calais and Somme départements, and that along Atlantic coasts.

Seille Valley

Work in the Seille valley goes back to the eighteenth century, which is when the term 'briquetage' was invented (referring to the mounds of brick-like material in the Marsal and Moyenvic areas – what we now know are the fired clay remnants of evaporation furnaces). Modern work started in the 1970s, but it was only with the creation of the latest programme of work in 2001 that the most spectacular results have emerged. As well as extensive survey by remote sensing and ground-based magnetometry, excavation at Marsal has produced enormous ranges of furnaces and other installations. Laurent Olivier has shown that there are two main phases of activity in the Seille valley: eighth to sixth centuries BC (Hallstatt C-D2), and second to first centuries BC (LaTène D); the industrial quantities of waste briquetage belong mainly to the late period (Olivier 2000 (2001); 2005). A typological development of the briquetage containers fits into this chronology (Olivier 2005: 222, figure 5) (Figure 18).

The fullest and most recent accounts of this work describe excavation at the Digues site in Marsal (Olivier 2010; 2015). Even though the excavation area

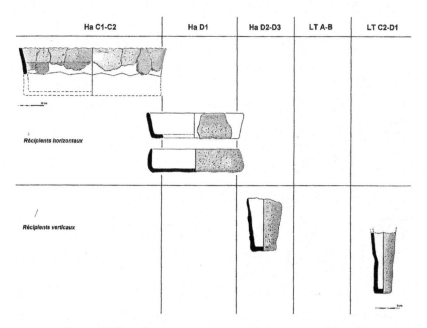

Figure 18 Development sequence of briquetage at Marsal.
Source: Olivier 2012.

was relatively small, large quantities of material were recovered, associated
with an extensive and highly complex stratigraphy. Production began in the
Hallstatt D1 period, around 600 BC, then in the next phase, dated to Ha D1–D2,
with nothing later, indicating it went out of use around 500 BC. A later stage
continues into modern times.

Detailed study of the material suggests a four-stage process in obtaining salt
from the brine: drawing out the brine, decanting and concentrating it, harvesting
the salt and shaping it into moulded blocks. A wooden bucket was probably used
in the first stage to draw the brine; for the second, the brine was decanted into
wattle and clay-lined pits, quadrangular in shape. Remains of braided cord were
found, believed to be a rope for hauling the brine from the wells into the
concentration pits. Once the brine was concentrated it was heated in order to
extract the salt as crystals; a series of small ovens with parallel rows of oval-
shaped combustion chambers were found; these heated large, flat-bottomed
basins of brine (Figure 19). Finally the crystalline salt was packed into moulds
and heated in furnaces, formed of rectangular pits topped by a briquetage rack
consisting of parallel clay bars.

Olivier estimates that in the earlier production phase, hundreds to thousands
of tonnes of salt may have been produced, but in the late phase this increased to
thousands to tens of thousands of tonnes (Olivier & Kovacik 2006: 564). The
scale of production was thus enormous, and can be considered industrial in
scale.

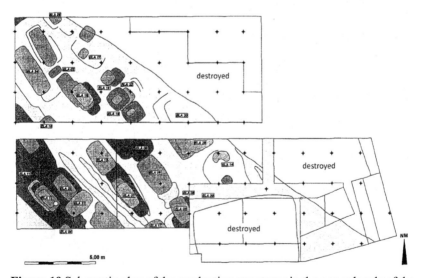

Figure 19 Schematic plan of the production structures in the upper levels of the
excavated area at Marsal, la Digue. Source: Olivier 2010.

Atlantic and Channel Ccoasts

There is a long history of study of the salt-making sites along the western and north-western coasts of France. The work of Tessier and Gouletquer go back to the 1960s and 70s (Tessier 1960; Gouletquer 1969; 1970), and Jean-Claude Hocquet has produced a number of important studies (Hocquet 1986; 1994; 2001). These have shown that the briquetage of the area developed over the course of the Iron Age and into the Gallo-Roman period, while the intensity of production suggests that it became increasingly industrial in nature. Very large numbers of sites are known, certainly in the hundreds. The work of Marie-Yvane Daire and colleagues has confirmed this picture (Daire 1994; 2003). In some cases, it was salty mud that was exploited through leaching and filtering rather than brine or seawater. This has implications for the type of furnace employed, however, since the sand or mud would have to be removed after boiling and deposited elsewhere.

In the north of France rescue excavations have recovered extensive evidence of salt working, for instance at Sorrus near Etaples (Desfossés 2000: 215ff.). Here sunken oval hearths or furnaces were reconstructed as having the characteristic griddle form, onto which pans and trays were placed. Beside the hearth, wattle-lined wells and pits for storing brine were found; the wells had silted up and briquetage was found in the upper layers; Weller's study of the briquetage (in Desfossés 2000: 272ff.) showed that a standard range of forms was present, consisting of beakers (moulds), supports (pedestals) and so-called 'hand-bricks'; these are mini-pedestals, squeezed by hand and placed between two troughs or pans (in Britain called spacers or clips), and structural elements from the furnace lining and griddle. These sites cover a broad range in the late Iron Age according to the pottery recovered, including several parts of the La Tène period. Weller also identified a number of regional variants as well as a chronological development that spanned much of the later Iron Age.

On the Franco-Belgian border, work has uncovered briquetage over many decades, notably at De Panne and Bray-Dunes (Thoen 1975; Kerger 1999); more recently, excavation at Steene-Pitgam has recovered an extensive assemblage of material, including briquetage, attributed to the Menapii tribe (Hannois 1999).

At sites near Abbeville, comparable installations have been found, for instance at Pont-Remy (Prilaux 2000). In Normandy, a range of sites have been found along the coasts of Lower Normandy, from the Mont-Saint-Michel bay, around the Cotentin peninsula, and along the north coast to the Seine (Carpentier *et al.* 2012), with a development over time from furnaces with slabs surmounted by pedestals supporting cylindrical containers at the time of the Hallstatt-La Tène transition around 450 BC, to a range of types involving troughs, hand-bricks (clips), and eventually griddle constructions during the successive centuries of La Tène. The estuary of Dives-sur-Mer has produced some of the earliest examples of this technology, notably at the site of la Vignerie, and around them animal bones and shells in great profusion (Carpentier & Marcigny 2019: 144).

In Brittany, a large collection of sites producing briquetage are known. Gouletquer (1970) identified a range of briquetage forms (such as trumpet-shaped, T-shaped and tripod pedestals) and was able to show how widespread the griddle-type of furnace that supported moulds was. All these sites consist of a furnace, with wells for obtaining water and storage pits for brine, though the specific layout may vary from site to site and area to area. In Aquitaine, the Marais Poitevin and the Saintonge area are particularly prolific in briquetage sites.

Spain

Among many recent studies in Spain, one in Valencia province may be mentioned: this focuses on the Requena-Utiel region between the rivers Cabriel and Magro, where there are numerous salt evaporation ponds and many salt toponyms, as well as the salt mine of Minglanilla. In some of these places, Iron Age (Iberian) material has been found, suggesting a close connection between settlement and salt production (Quixal Santos 2020). Pliny (*Natural History* 31, 39: 80) refers to the salt mine at Egelesta, where the 'salt is cut into almost transparent blocks'; this place name may be a Latin version of Iberian 'Ikalkusken' or 'Ikalesken', a town which produced coinage in the Republican period and which is believed to lie in Cuenca province. This identification is, however, disputed: Jonathan Terán Manrique (2017) points out that Pliny refers to rock salt, not brine salt, so that a location near the mines of Minglanilla-La Pesquera is more likely.

Elsewhere, much attention has been given over recent years to the commerce in salt in inland Iberia in the Iron Age and Roman periods. Given the large number of sources, both rock salt and brine, this is hardly surprising. Jonathan Terán Manrique (2015) has considered the productive potential of a series of thirty-three saltworks in north-west Spain in the Iron Age, on the basis of altitude, assumed temperature and precipitation at different times, demonstrating that between the eighth and first centuries BC there was considerable variation, but that an area of around 78 km^2 is where all the optimal factors coalesce, centring on Atienza y Sigüenza and containing ten saltworks.

The fact that coastal southern and eastern Spain was the target of Phoenician colonisation has led to speculation about the need for salt in the settlements founded in this way, even though no specific evidence in the form of salt boiling debris has been found (Martínez Mangato 2012).

Germany

In Germany, a number of areas have provided extensive evidence for salt production in the Iron Age, with Bad Nauheim in Hesse the most informative. Earlier accounts of this important group of sites (Kull 2003) have now been superceded by a definitive publication of the excavations in Kurstrasse in 2001–04 (Hansen 2016). This shows how remarkable and extensive the evidence from the town is.

Extensive salt workings in historical times have forerunners in the Roman period and the Iron Age. The brine springs contain 2–4 per cent salt. Numerous evaporation furnaces have turned up, whole or partial, with extensive areas of burning; much was early medieval in date, including stone troughs, wooden tanks and lead collection pans. The Roman interest in Bad Nauheim salt is attested by circular collection areas made of wattle in the area of the southern saltworks (Kull 2003: 140–1, Abb. 65–67). In the southern part of town, salt-related installations included wattle fences, wooden box-like shafts, channels, troughs and portable objects. Isolated finds of briquetage (pedestals, beakers) show that this method was also used.

In Kurstrasse, a large area was opened and a remarkable series of installations discovered, dated to various phases of La Tène (B2/C1 through to D2, the third to first centuries BC); this was supported by a significant number of dendro dates falling in the first centuries BC and AD). There was a remarkable series of stone paved areas, roughly square (Figure 20), along with channelling, wattle fences, and wooden troughs. A series of hearths or ovens lay in some of these enclosures, while wooden boxes were probably used to store the brine. Leif Hansen's work on the records has described how the brine was collected in basins or boxes, in which at least four chronologically different construction types were in evidence. In the east of the excavation area, clay-lined basins surrounded by wattle fencing came to light. The water evaporated through the heat of the sun or the effects of wind, increasing the salt content of the brine. There were larger numbers of carefully constructed paved areas, sloping towards the middle, and surrounded by a bank of mixed ash and earth. Small wooden boxes, integrated into the surrounding bank, with an outlet in the direction of the paving, were part of this arrangement. The brine was first filled into the wooden boxes, so that the sulphur and impurities could sink, and then fed into the paved installations. A range of roughly rectangular, loaf-shaped or bottle-shaped oven chambers, with two or three openings on the long and

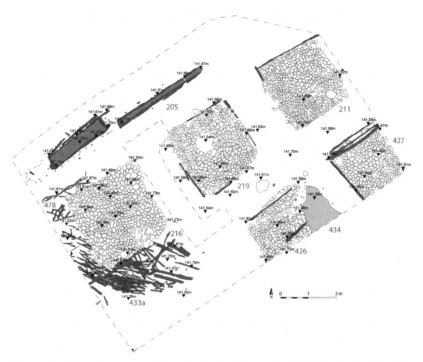

Figure 20 Plan of one part of the site in the Kurstraße, Bad Nauheim, showing some of the many stone paved areas on the site used for brine evaporation.
Source: Hansen 2016.

Drawing: V. Grünewald, Mainz, reproduction courtesy of LfDH, hessenARCHÄOLOGIE.

narrow sides for the firing and heating or draught regulation, were recorded. The boiling vessels stood on clay supports, into which brine was repeatedly introduced. At 26 per cent salinity the salt [crystals] emerged. Large quantities of broken vessels show that they were broken to get the salt out. The whole process was systematically planned (Hansen 2016: 127–8).

This description of the process at Bad Nauheim is remarkable for its detail, a consequence of the excellent preservation on the site. As Hansen remarks, were other towns as extensively excavated, no doubt similar things would be found on them. At Schwäbisch Hall, east of Heilbronn, for instance, a range of installations was found, including wattle-lined brine storage pits and wooden troughs, the largest being 5 m long, 1.2 m wide and 50 cm deep (Simon 1995: 79ff.). Opinions have varied over how these troughs functioned; earlier ideas were that they were intended as some kind of grading device for concentrating brine, perhaps by means of inserting heated ceramic pieces (which were indeed found inside some of them). As well as these wooden objects, large quantities of briquetage were found, mainly containers, slabs, and conical or triangular-section supports.

Sachsen-Anhalt continued to produce salt, with briquetage in evidence in a number of sites (survey of the evidence: Ettel *et al.* 2018). Particularly important is the Brehna site, considered for its Early Bronze Age evidence, but also prolific in briquetage in the Late Bronze and Early Iron Age, from Ha A2/B1 through to Ha D (von Rauchhaupt & Schunke 2010) (Figure 17). Pedestals and cylindrical columns, and a pit full of crucibles, were concentrated in a number of areas of the site, notably those with large houses and halls; firedogs were also frequent and some may have been used as part of evaporation furnaces. Some of the well-preserved subrectangular ovens contained briquetage (columns); others did not. Since the outlines of several post-built houses were found in one part of the site, the excavators have speculated whether at least one of them (House 4) might represent the house of a salt-worker.

The area round Erdeborn, west of Halle, is prolific in briquetage sites. This is an important area for salt production since the Salzige See (Salty Lake) was situated here (it disappeared in the nineteenth century as a result of copper mining and subsequent drainage operations; only small pools remain of this 9 km^2 lake). Survey and excavation on the outskirts of Erdeborn in 2002–6 revealed numerous pits and burnt areas, with abundant briquetage (Ipach 2016). This mainly consists of columns of various kinds, crucibles, and clay lumps or balls which were used either to fix the crucible to the column or stabilise the column base (Figure 21). An attempt at quantifying the amount of salt produced in the excavated part of the site, on the basis of the capacity of the crucibles, the number of pedestals (each supporting one crucible) and the specific gravity of salt, led to an estimate of 733 kg of salt from the excavated area – originally more since the actual area of production was probably greater.

Recent excavations in the Paulusviertel, one of the suburbs of Halle, have produced large amounts of briquetage on an early Iron Age settlement site (Petzschmann 2015). Since much of Halle lies over ancient salt production areas, this comes as little surprise.

Other parts of Germany where Iron Age salt production is attested include Werl, Kreis Soest, in Westphalia (Leidinger 1996; Laumann 2000), while it is highly likely that the rich salt sources of the north of the country, for instance around Lüneburg, were also exploited in later prehistory.

Other Parts of Northern Europe

There is evidence in Poland, too, for the Iron Age production of salt, for instance in Inowrocław (Bednarczyk *et al.* 2015), where many hearths and

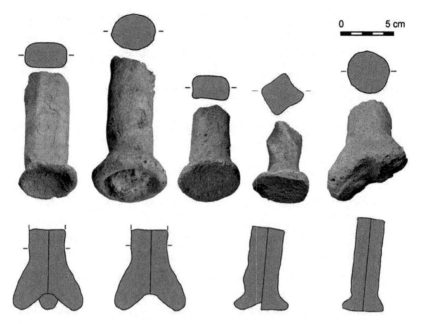

Figure 21 Briquetage from Erdeborn, district Mansfeld-Südharz. Source: Ettel,
Ipach and Schneider 2018,
courtesy of Professor Peter Ettel.

a brine well were discovered, complete with a stepped ladder made from a pine
trunk. The excavators believe that other wooden installations formed part of
a graduation tower, such as has been reconstructed in the park where the sites
are located.

In the Netherlands, sites used for salt production have been studied by Peter
van den Broeke, who has charted the production and movement of salt using
specific forms of briquetage in the lower Rhine area, on both the coast and
inland (van den Broeke 1995; 2007). This movement reached as far inland as the
brown coal area between Aachen and Cologne (Simons 1987).

Britain

In Britain, the 'Red Hills' of the eastern coast of England have long been known
to archaeologists. They are especially well known from the Essex coast as well
as other parts of East Anglia, and the north Kent coast (Miles 1975); they have
been the subject of several reviews, notably by Warwick Rodwell (1979),
A. J. Fawn and others (1990), and Paul Sealey (1995). The lack of distinctive
pottery on such sites often makes dating difficult. Rodwell and Fawn *et al.*

considered some forty-eight sites where there was dating evidence, concluding that twenty-eight dated to the Iron Age and twenty to the Roman period, mostly early in that period (first century AD). Sealey shows that dating based on pottery and coins centres on the first century AD, with some evidence of a late Roman reoccupation on certain sites (Sealey 1995: 76).

Typically a saltern of this kind consists of a low mound on a coastal flat, its reddish colour a result of abundant fired brick-like material (briquetage), along with ash and charcoal. Excavation has generally produced hearths or ovens, storage tanks and settling pits. A typical example of such a site is that at Helpringham Fen in Lincolnshire (Bell *et al.* 1999). This site produced abundant briquetage in the form of bricks and plates, pyramidal pieces, props, bridges, bars and vessel fragments, associated with rectangular hearths surrounded by ditches, with much ash and other firing debris. The associated pottery dates to the third century BC, with later Iron Age and Roman material in the upper layers, suggesting continuity.

There are dozens of such sites that one could list, though few give really detailed information on construction, use and functioning. Recent excavation in advance of the London Gateway development, however, is an exception. Here the excavators found much evidence of salt production, with numerous salterns of both Iron Age and Roman date (Biddulph *et al.* 2012; Biddulph 2013), a significant number dated to the Roman period, both early and late. The early Roman production was less extensive than that in the Iron Age, but the presence of ditches, pits and postholes, associated with first century pottery, shows that it was present.

In the later Roman period, salt working expanded considerably. There was a Roman presence in the second and earlier third centuries, with a small amount of briquetage, but in the third and fourth centuries salt making became a major industry (Biddulph *et al.* 2012: chap. 6). The salterns generally consisted of a subrectangular space defined by u-shaped ditches at either end, with a hearth and settling tank inside, with additional pits and drainage channels (Figure 22). One case was an exceptionally well-preserved tile-built structure, the hearth consisting of a circular chamber with a flue attached, giving it a keyhole shape. A more unusual structure was round, defined by encircling ditches, with an internal diameter of 13 m, also containing a hearth and a settling tank. A large amount (167 kg) of briquetage was present, consisting of troughs, bowls and moulds, as well as firebars, pedestals, wedges and a range of moulded supports and stabilisers, in addition to shapeless furnace lining fragments. These finds, and their publication, represent a major addition to the known corpus of Roman salt-making material in north-west Europe.

In Norfolk, sites are also quite common, though most are medieval. One Roman example is that at Middleton near King's Lynn, where a subrectangular

Figure 22 Hypothetical reconstruction of Late Roman salt making at the Stanford Wharf Nature Reserve, showing a composite of elements from different salterns.

Drawing: Mark Gridley, reproduction courtesy of Oxford Archaeology (South).

enclosure with oven and settling tank was found, along with extensive brique-tage and late Roman pottery (Crowson 2001).

In Lincolnshire, the situation has recently been reviewed by Tom Lane (2018: 99–110), following on from the earlier assessment he conducted with Elaine Morris (Lane & Morris 2001). While a number of the sites in that county belong to the Bronze to Middle Iron Ages, many more come from the late Iron Age and continue into the early Roman period. This is particularly true in the Spalding area, where a series of sites span the first centuries BC and AD. Lane espouses the argument by Alastair Strang that the place name Salinae in Ptolemy's *Geography* that is usually associated with Droitwich (see the following) in fact refers to the area around Skegness on the Lincolnshire coast (Strang 1997: 23); this would certainly suggest that Lincolnshire was a major salt production area in the Roman period. The South Lincolnshire Fenland sites extend southwards into the Cambridgeshire Fens, where some sites appear to be of Late Iron Age or Romano-British date (Lane *et al.* 2019).

The county of Cheshire in the north of the English Midlands is home to the largest salt deposits in the country, with extensive evidence of salt production in historical times. The suffix 'wich', found in several place names on the Cheshire salt field, refers not, as in other places, to the Anglo-Saxon 'wic' (from Latin *vicus*) but specifically to a connection with salt (allegedly from Old Norse 'vik', bay, where salt might be collected).

Excavations at Nantwich have uncovered remarkable survivals of Roman salt production (Arrowsmith & Power 2012). Brine was collected in tanks formed of stout wooden uprights and planks and lined with clay (Figure 23), with dendro dates in the 130s AD, and a similar but smaller chamber; later, in the third–fourth centuries these were replaced by smaller wicker-lined pits. The actual evaporation process was centred on a series of nearby hearths.

As well as Nantwich, salt production has a long history at both Northwich and Middlewich; all three towns are close to the modern salt mines at Winsford. As discussed in the following, the place name Salinae is applied to a locality in this area, indicating Roman salt production. At Middlewich, a brine evaporation hearth, a timber-lined well and a wattle-lined pit, dating to the first centuries BC and AD, were excavated along with a sizeable quantity of briquetage (Bestwick 1975; Williams & Reid 2008) (Figure 24). Excavations over many years have confirmed a major Roman presence in the town, notably military in the form of a fort, along with brine kilns and hearths, and a great deal of briquetage. An inscribed lead salt pan has also been found (D. Garner in Nevell & Fielding 2004–5); others are known from Cheshire (Penney & Shotter 1996).

Figure 23 Brine tank from Nantwich, Cheshire. Source: Arrowsmith & Power 2012.

Figure 24 Briquetage from Roman Middlewich. Source: Nevell 2005, courtesy of Leigh Dodd.

Droitwich in Worcestershire is believed to be the Salinae listed in the Ravenna Cosmography,[5] and is historically an important salt town. The brine at Droitwich is highly salt-saturated (25 per cent). Excavation at the Old Bowling Green site recovered plentiful briquetage associated with brine tanks lined with clay and oak boards or stakes, and hearths (Woodiwiss 1992: chap. 2). In the Roman period there was an extensive Roman presence in and around Droitwich, including a fort and a well-appointed villa (Hurst 2006). In the second century AD, a large post and plank structure was recorded near what became a medieval brine well (Hurst 1997), probably part of a mechanism for large-scale extraction of brine. The excavator suggests that this indicates an expansion of salt production in the area, perhaps with the industry becoming subject to imperial control, as happened elsewhere in the Roman world. Interestingly, briquetage is no longer found when this occurred, so the technology changed, presumably to the use of lead pans, such as are known from elsewhere. A nearby timber complex is interpreted as a possible lifting device, dating to later in the second century. These activities appear to have ceased by

---

[5] Though it seems not the one listed by Ptolemy (see Section 6).

the third century, but the area again became the centre of salt production in the medieval period.

One of the most important aspects of salt production and distribution in the area covering the Midlands, as far north as Cheshire, and the Welsh Marches, is the presence of specific pottery types that were created in order to transport the resulting salt. This coarse ceramic, known as Very Coarse Pottery (VCP), has been identified on a series of Midland and Welsh sites, and was particularly used for salt from Cheshire sources (Morris 1985; 1994; Nevell & Fielding 2004–5). The distribution of these types has been supplemented by the work of Janice Kinory (2012: 32ff.), who has argued that most salt was distributed in archaeologically invisible containers, since so many Iron Age sites have no sign of briquetage, even where it might be expected on other grounds.

Another area of intense activity in the Roman period was Somerset in south-west England (Leech 1977; 1981; Grove & Brunning 1998; Hughes *et al.* 2017). Four areas of the county were identified by Grove and Brunning as particularly important, some near the sea, others further inland; the early Roman ones are nearer the sea, the later ones further inland, which they interpret as indicating a marine transgression that made the sites nearer the sea unworkable.

An area of particularly dense activity was that on the low-lying Somerset Levels north-east of Bridgwater (Rippon 2007). One of these sites near Woolavington, recently excavated, produced the typical features of such a saltern mound, with pits, settling tanks and channels, with abundant briquetage (containers, bars, stabilisers, slabs and structural fragments) (Hughes *et al.* 2017). The brine was evaporated on hearths dug into the ground, with a simple superstructure. A platform was constructed of bars and slabs, onto which lead containers were placed for the boiling process, lead apparently being preferred to clay, since there were few clay containers.

Salt was also produced on the south coast of England in the Iron Age and Roman periods. The area around Poole Harbour seems to have been important for salt production (e.g. Farrar 1975)[6] while Christchurch Harbour might be another significant spot, given the presence of briquetage on the major site at Hengistbury Head (Poole 1987) and the quite short distance from there to Danebury, where briquetage was also found.

As well as these parts of southern and central England, where the presence of salt working sites has long been known, recent years have seen the discovery of briquetage on sites in the north-east of England, though at present it appears that these are restricted to the late Iron Age and early Roman period (Willis 2016) and there is no certain evidence that it continued beyond the first century AD. This is

---

[6] I thank Janice Kinory for pointing out the potential significance of Poole Harbour.

true both of Stanwick (the subject of Willis's study) and of the site at Scotch Corner, not far away, the largest assemblage of briquetage from the region (Charlotte Britton, 'Briquetage', in Fell 2020: 456–7). It is interesting and somewhat puzzling, however, that few of these sites are on the coast where the boiling process presumably took place; an exception is the Needles Eye enclosure at Berwick on Tweed, from an Iron Age context (Proctor 2012). The briquetage found must represent the transport of salt in its containers around the communities of the inland Late Iron Age and early Roman period, without any clear evidence of the production sites being available.

6 Greek and Roman Salt in the Mediterranean

It is well known that salt played an important part in the life and economy of the ancient world. We know that the English word 'salary' comes from Latin *salarium*, the sum paid to soldiers allegedly for the purchase of salt; and that the Via Salaria ran from Rome (originally from the mouth of the Tiber) across Italy to *Castrum Truentinum* (Porto d'Ascoli) on the Adriatic coast, connecting two important salt-production areas of the Roman world. While this suggests extensive knowledge of salt in the Roman and Greek worlds, things are rather more complicated than this.

For the Greek and Roman periods, literary sources are of course available to complement the archaeological ones. This might be thought to be an inestimable advantage, but while it does add considerably to our knowledge, it also adds frustrations, because on the one hand some authors (notably Pliny the Elder) tell us a lot about where salt was found but little about how it was produced, and on the other the indications about production in some of the sources are not easy to understand. Nevertheless, it is essential to make use of the texts as far as possible in order to obtain a full picture of the position of salt in the economy of the Graeco-Roman world.

Here I shall consider what the ancient authors tell us, insofar as it gives useful information from an archaeological point of view; and then move to consider what archaeological evidence there is for salt production in the Graeco-Roman world, specifically in Europe. The evidence consists above all of indications of coastal production in pans and lagoons, particularly in Italy and Spain (but also other areas such as Anatolia). I must also mention Roman interests in production from inland rock salt and brine sources, notably from parts of Romania where site and artefactual evidence is supplemented by inscriptions (also present in Italy).

A lot of what survives from the available Roman sources, both literary and archaeological, relates to matters such as administration and taxation, which I cannot cover here. It is also the case that salt was much used in the production of fish-sauce, *garum*, also beyond my present scope but a preoccupation of many modern writers on Roman salt.

Literary Sources

Full lists of references to and excellent discussions of the ancient authors have been provided by three scholars, Cristina Carusi (2008), Bernard Moinier and Olivier Weller (2015). I shall therefore only allude here to particular sources that shed useful light on production between the sixth century BC and the fourth century AD.

Pliny the Elder (AD 23/4–79) provides the fullest account of the locations of salt working in the ancient literature, its uses, and something about methods of production (*Natural History* Book XXXI, 73–92). His words have been reproduced many times and only the most indicative need to be repeated here. It is frustrating that he says little about exactly how production proceeded, other than to indicate that solar evaporation was the main technique used:

> All salt is artificial or native; each is formed in several ways, but there are two agencies, condensation or drying up of water. It is dried out of the Tarentine lake by summer sun, when the whole pool turns into salt, although it is always shallow, never exceeding knee height, likewise in Sicily from a lake, called Cocanicus, and from another near Gela. Of these the edges only dry up; in Phrygia, Cappadocia, and at Aspendus, the evaporation is wider, in fact right to the centre. There is yet another wonderful thing about it: the same amount is restored during the night as is taken away during the day. All salt from pools is fine powder, and not in blocks.[7]
>
> Of artificial salt there are various kinds. The usual one, and the most plentiful, is made in salt pools by running into them sea water not without streams of fresh water, but rain helps very much, and above all much <warm> sunshine, without which it does not dry out. In Africa around Utica are formed heaps of salt like hills; when they have hardened under sun and moon, they are not melted by any moisture, and even iron cuts them with difficulty. It is also however made in Crete without fresh water by letting the sea flow into the pools, and around Egypt by the sea itself, which penetrates the soil, soaked as I believe it is, by the Nile. Salt is also made by pouring water from wells into salt pools.

[These passages indicate that solar evaporation in coastal lagoons was a principal method used. There are (or were) several salt production sites near Taranto, notably the Salina grande and Salina piccolo, south-east of the city, and many smaller *saline* in the area (digilander.libero.it/antonio1956/saline.htm, last accessed 25 January 2021); the Cocanicus lake in Sicily has not been identified, but the salt lagoons and pans of the west coast are still in production. On Crete there were salt pans in production at Elounda on the north coast until 1972.]

---

[7] Loeb edition, translated by W. H. S. Jones, 1921.

> In Chaonia there is a spring, from which they boil water, and on cooling obtain a salt that is insipid and not white.

[An indication of brine boiling. Ancient Chaonia lies in northern Epirus and southern Albania. The spring in question has not been identified.]

> In the provinces of Gaul and Germany they pour salt water on burning logs ... I find in Theophrastus that the Umbrians were wont to boil down in water the ash of reeds and rushes, until only a very little liquid remained. Moreover, from the liquor of salted foods salt is recovered by reboiling, and when evaporation is complete its saline character is regained.

[Salt produced by throwing brine onto burning wood or ashes]

> Salt-pools have reached their highest degree of purity in what may be called embers of salt, which is the lightest and whitest of its kind.
>
> Besides these salines there is also what is called at the salt-pools *salpugo*, or sometimes *salsilago*. It is entirely liquid, differing from sea brine by its more salty character.

[Further information about the results of brine evaporation.]

Brief mentions of salt pans and lakes are found in several other authors; I have listed the most obvious of these in an earlier work (Harding 2013: 135–9).

As discussed in Section 2, two authors give significantly more information about the production of salt in pans, Rutilius Namatianus (late fourth century AD) and Marcus Manilius (earlier first century AD). Although neither was concerned with salt as such, the incidental information they provide is of great value and is confirmed by what happens in modern salt pans.

A number of authors have used the indications of the ancient authors to estimate production volumes at various times and places in the Roman world (reviewed by Saile 2015). The figures are large; 350,000 tonnes per annum according to Bernard Moinier (Moinier 2011). This shows very clearly that production must have been taking place at many of the places identified as possible sources. Much is also known from inscriptions, surviving fragments of writing (e.g. the Vindolanda tablets) and literary sources about the price and economic value of salt at various times (Stockinger 2015).

The Location of Salt Pans and Lagoons Potentially Used in Ancient Times

Greece

There are significant salt pans today in many places in Greece: on Kos, for instance, at Tigaki, 10 km from the ancient city of Kos (less to some of the surviving parts of the city); at Mesolongi on the north side of the Gulf of Corinth;

and at Alykes near Katastari on Zakynthos. None of these is mentioned in the ancient authors, nor do they have evidence for ancient working, but other pans are mentioned (Pliny). Strabo, for instance, in his *Geography* (IX, 21–2) refers to salt lakes, quarries, pans and marshes in many places in the Greek world. Of particular interest are those in Attica, which would have supplied Athens. Two demes containing the name Halai (salt works) are Alaieis or Halaieis, believed to be on the west coast at present-day Voula, and Halai Araphenidis, believed to lie close to modern Artemida where there was formerly a salt lake (now disappeared through the urbanisation of the area). Xenophon (*Hellenica* II, 4, 30, 34) mentions the 'salt plain' (Halipedon), and the 'mud' of the Halai (presumably the salt marsh) that is inland from Piraeus. Another Halai lay in Boeotia (Pausanias, *Description of Greece*, 9.4.25). None of these places preserves evidence of ancient working but the areas in question are very likely those that were used in ancient times.

Tragasai in the Troad (north-west Anatolia) lies close to the modern town of Tuzla which lies on salt formations (tuz = salt in Turkish), but the only mention of a connection with salt comes from a fragment of the Greek historian Phylarchos, who refers to an episode when King Lysimachos imposed and then removed a tax from the salt, which had previously been free for all to collect. Tuzla lies on the modern river Tuzla Çayı, presumably named for its salty character, and flowing through the *halesion pedion* (salty plain). The Tragasai saltworks were well known in antiquity, and Carusi has quoted values for production in the nineteenth century AD, as well as for Thermisi in the Argolid, and for the small island of Kausos (Gavdos) off the southern coast of Crete (Carusi 2015: 344; 2018: 484).

Other literary or epigraphic evidence relates to individuals who had concerns in the salt industry, or economic activity related to it (Carusi 2006), but these do not help with the identification of salt production sites. They do, however, reinforce the general picture of how important salt was in ancient Greek social and economic life.

Italy

For Italy, the ancient authors make reference to the importance of salt in early Rome (to say nothing of the situation in later times). Livy, for instance, refers to the creation of the Ostia saltworks (below), and also to the situation in 508 BC, at the time of the Etruscan occupation of Rome, when 'the monopoly of salt, the price of which was very high, was taken out of the hands of individuals and wholly assumed by the government' (*History* II. ix. 6); and later, during the Carthaginian Wars in 204 BC, the censors established a new system for the production and distribution of salt using private contractors, thus bringing in a revenue to the exchequer (*History* XXIX. xxxvii. 3–4). These are special circumstances in the context of a city that was already highly developed; but there are many places where Iron Age coastal settlement was surely involved in the production of salt. The Phoenician site of Motya, for instance, on a small island off the west coast of Sicily, is very close to the extensive salt pans both on the nearby mainland, and on the Isole dello Stagnone (Figure 25). Close by, Trápani, ancient Drepana/Drepanum, lies directly beside extensive pans, while Marsala (ancient Lilybaeum), a Carthaginian settlement, lies only a few kilometres to the south. One could repeat this story in many other places: for instance on the Adriatic coast of Italy, where the enormous salt pans at Margherita di Savoia, near Trinitápoli, lie near the ancient sites of Salapia/Salpi and Bardulos/Barulum (modern Barletta), the name being of Phoenician origin. The salt pans at Cervia lie midway between the ancient cities of Ravenna and Ariminum (Rimini). One could repeat this situation in many other parts of the Mediterranean, for instance at Nin (ancient Aenona) on the Dalmatian coast north of Zadar. In all these cases it is not possible to provide definitive proof that Iron Age peoples actively utilised the salt, but it would be very strange if they did not.

Figure 25 Salt pans of the Marsala lagoon.

Photo: Sapienza University of Rome, Motya Expedition, courtesy of Professor Lorenzo Nigro.

Salinae

The Latin word for saltworks is *salinae*; this place name occurs in several places in the Roman world, though since the word simply refers to a place where salt was produced it is principally an indicator of function. Obviously all such places must have lain on or beside a salt source, whether the sea, brine springs, or a rock salt massif. Cicero referred to inland saltworks.[8] Thus the designation of Middlewich, Cheshire, as Salinae in the Ravenna Cosmography refers to the importance of that area for salt production; 'Salinis' lies between *Derventio* and *Condate* in the list, which places it in the Cheshire salt area, either Middlewich or Nantwich (from this it is clear that the name is functional rather than traditional). Another Salinis is listed in the Cosmography near Vertis (probably Worcester) and has usually been identified with Droitwich, while the *Geography* of Ptolemy includes a third, which is identified by Strang (1997) with the Skegness area of Lincolnshire, though Spalding, where a number of saltern sites have been found (Lane 2018: 73–8), seems another possibility.[9] This, however, depends on a particular interpretation of the sometimes-baffling indications of the ancient geographers; there has been much discussion of the possibilities over the years and none is completely secure. What is clear, however, is that there were several Roman saltworks in the English Midlands.

Outside Britain, places called Salinae occur in the southern part of the province of Gallia, where, according to Ptolemy, it was the chief town of the Suetrii (from inscriptions believed to be Castellane in the Alpes Maritimes: Bérard & Barruol 1997: 116–18: 553); and at Ocna Mureş in Alba county in Romania, named in the Tabula Peutingeriana between Patavissa (Potaissa, today's Turda) and Apulum (Alba Iulia); the name probably refers to the Roman fort at nearby Războieni-Cetate rather than the medieval and modern settlement of Ocna Mureş itself. The Tabula Peutingeriana shows other places named Salinae. Leaving aside those in North Africa, one refers to a place on the Adriatic coast just north of Pescara (Aternum), probably connected with the river Salinus (now Saline); another is on the coast further south, at Salapia/ Salpi – which must refer to the pans of Trinitápoli.[10]

---

[8] '*salinae ab ora maritima remotissimae*', Cicero *De natura deorum*, II, 132.

[9] 'Then the Katueuchlanoi [presumed to be Catuvellauni], among whom the towns Salinai, Ourolanion [Verulamium]' (Ptolemy, *Geography*, 2,3,21). Lincolnshire is not usually included in the territory of the Catuvellauni so Strang has to extend their territory northwards to make this fit. He excludes Droitwich as a possible candidate.

[10] In Vigo, Galicia, north-west Spain, the museum that presents the salterns has been given the name Salinae.

This information is useful but hardly definitive, since many locations that could have been called Salinae were not, or were only given the generic name rather than a specifically recorded one. When this information is combined with that from inscriptions, however, more can be said, because there were specific individuals who were responsible for the work at the various sites. These are recorded as *conductores salinarum*, which might be loosely translated as salt works 'managers' – though in fact it is not known exactly what role these people played: since in a few cases (Micia, Domneşti, Apulum), the person was also responsible for *pascuus* (pasture), it seems they had other tasks than simply managing the production of salt. In some cases, an *actor* (agent) is mentioned, who may have had financial as well as managerial responsibilities. The administration of salt production, distribution and taxation was evidently a major concern in the Roman world, both in Italy and in the provinces, but much remains uncertain about it.

A very important inscription is that recovered during excavation and survey work in the *campus salinarum romanarum*, on the right bank of the Tiber on the site of the former Maccarese lagoon (now largely under Fiumicino airport). This lies at the *ager portuensis* near, but across the Tiber from, Ostia (Cébeillac-Gervasoni & Morelli 2014; Morelli & Forte 2014). These salterns were evidently for Rome's use, not for Ostia, which had its own works on the left side of the river. The site is very interesting in itself for the installations recovered in excavation. The *campus salinarum romanarum* is known from other inscriptions as well (Meiggs 1973: 268).

There are also six inscriptions in Romania (Dacia) which record the presence of *conductores salinarum* (Mihailescu-Bîrliba 2016, with references to earlier literature). As mentioned before, Romania is very rich in salt sources, which the Romans evidently exploited fully (Wollmann 1996). Not all the findspots of these inscriptions are known as salt production areas; some were evidently places where salt was stored – for instance, at the legionary fortress of Apulum. One example is that of Sânpaul in Harghita county (Figure 26A), where there is a Roman fort (from which the inscription in question came) and not far away salt springs, which have produced timbers of Iron Age and early modern date. Another is that of Domneşti (Figure 26B), close to the salt massif and former salt mine at Sărăţel in Bistriţa-Năsăud county (Wollmann 1996: 249, 413 Pl. CX). Wollmann has considered the question of Roman salt production in Dacia in some detail; the epigraphic material is the clearest evidence for a major Roman interest in salt in the province.

At present, no inscriptions are known from other countries recording these *conductores*, but given the frequency of the designation Salinae it would come as no surprise if more turned up.

A)   B)

Figure 26A and B *(A)* Roman altar from between Sânpaul and Ocland,
Harghita county, Romania. Photo: Petru Palamar, National Museum of the
Eastern Carpathians, Sfântu Gheorghe, courtesy of Valeriu Cavruc.
Transcription: Soli invicto pro salute C. Iuli Valentini c(onductoris) salinar(um)
C. Iulius Omucio libertus actor posuit
(Caius Iulius Omucio, freedman, *actor* [agent], set up [this altar] to the
unconquered sun[god] for the wellbeing of Caius Iulius Valentinus, *conductor*
of saltworks). Muzeul Naţional Secuiesc, Sfântu Gheorghe. Photo: Petru
Palamar, courtesy of Valeriu Cavruc. *(B)* Roman altar from Domneşti,
Bistriţa-Năsăud county, Romania. Photo: Valeriu Cavruc. Transcription: I(ovi)
O(ptimo) M(aximo) et I(unoni) M(inervae) *or* I(nvicto)
M(ithrae)pro sal(u)t(e) Ael(i) Mari fl(aminis) col(oniae) conduc(toris) pasc(ui)
e(t) salina(rum) Atticus act(or) eius v(otam) s(olvit) l(ibens) m(erito)
(dedicated to Jupiter, Juno and Minerva (or Mithras) by Atticus, the *actor* of
Aelius Marius, priest of the colony, and *conductor* of the pasture and saltworks).
Muzeul Judeţean, Bistriţa. Photo: Valeriu Cavruc.

Archaeological Evidence

Until recently, there was little direct archaeological evidence for salt production of Roman date in the Mediterranean world (discussion of saltworks round the Mediterranean before the start of recent investigations: Traina 1992). As discussed previously, it was and is assumed that modern salt pans continued the activities of ancient ones without any specific ancient material being present. Now, however, work in both Italy and Spain has changed that situation (recent review: García Vargas & Maganto 2017).

Work in advance of the construction of Fiumicino airport uncovered a range of installations in the former Maccarese lake (Morelli & Forte 2014; Grossi *et al.* 2015), near the coast south-west of Rome and opposite the ancient city of Ostia. A series of channels were built in order to create a 'hydraulic system'. The most remarkable of these was a 1 km long 'dam' of amphorae, no less than 1,439 in number, placed vertically in the ground, their mouths likely to have projected above the level of the ground; they were probably placed in a raised bank. At places along its length walled channels cut it, and while the precise way in which the system worked is hypothetical, the excavators compare it with the description by Georgius Agricola in *De Re Metallica* (1556) of the method of creating a coastal saltwork (cf the account of the Vigo saltworks given by Currás in the following). The whole might have functioned by letting salt water into the pans at the start of summer, closing the sluices, and distributing the water across the various enclosed spaces. The amphora dam served both as a barrier and as a means of preventing the unwanted ingress of more seawater.

The foundation of Ostia is associated, according to Livy, with the rise of Rome during the reign of Ancus Martius (640–616 BC).[11] These works were on the left (south) side of the Tiber, and probably north of the Rome road, around 1 km east of the town (Meiggs 1973: 19). Once Rome had conquered the Etruscan city of Veii in 396 BC, it was possible to establish the saltworks on the right side of the river (above). Studies of the Ostia saltworks have relied on literary references for many years, showing that salt was one of the reasons for the rise of Rome (Giovannini 1985; 2001); estimates of the annual output, by comparison with the quantities from similar saltworks of the medieval period, lie between 15,000 and 20,000 tonnes, bringing in a huge sum to the Roman treasury once the works had been brought into public hands. Nothing remains of the saltworks at Ostia today, since they were abandoned in the nineteenth century, but historical maps show where the salt lagoon lay, north-east of the town (Pannuzi 2013) (Figure 27).

---

[11] 'At the Tiber's mouth the city of Ostia was founded, and salt-works were established nearby', Livy, *Histories* I.XXXIII.9, trans. B. O. Foster, Loeb Classical Library 114. Cambridge, MA: Harvard University Press, 1919.

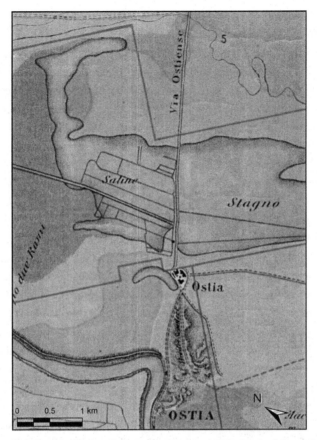

Figure 27 Map of 1884 showing the Ostia area, with the position of the town and its *salinae*. Source Huijzendveld (n.d.), *Creative Commons License* **CC BY-NC-SA 4.0.**

The location of the saltworks of Pompeii (which were, according to a reference in the Roman writer on agriculture Columella, dedicated to Hercules[12]), is conjectural, but they are believed to lie on the old coastline around 1 km west of the town (Murolo 1995). This conjecture is supported by the existence of Oscan inscriptions referring to *veru sarinu – porta salina* in Latin – probably to be identified with the later Herculaneum gate at the north-western edge of the town, and thus leading to the saltworks. The marsh would

---

[12] Quae dulcis Pompeia palus vicina salinis Herculeis – 'where the sweet Pompeian marsh / To Herculean salt-pits neighbour lies', Columella *De Re Rustica* X, 132, referring to the planting of cabbages; trans. E. S. Forster, Edward H. Heffner, Loeb Classical Library 408. Cambridge, MA: Harvard University Press, 1955.

thus lie around the whole of the area to the south and south-west, as far as the river Sarno and the former bay (Murolo 1995: 117, Tab. XLII).

At Volterra in Tuscany, the saltworks at Saline di Volterra are modern but the salt may well have been exploited in ancient times. The account by Rutilius Namatianus is concerned with the coast at Vada around 15 km to the west, which may have been the main source of salt for Etruscan and Roman Volterra.

Many other places along the Tyrrhenian coast of Italy are actual or potential ancient salt sites. These have been listed by Carusi, among others (2008: 316–17, figs. 1–2). Thus Etruscan cities such as Populonia and Tarquinia must have had salt production sites on the coast, even if their remains today are slight or invisible. These matters have also been considered by Alessandri and colleagues (Alessandri *et al.* 2019).

For the Adriatic, although there are many current or former saltworks, there has been little modern archaeological work to investigate whether traces of ancient working survive. An exception is work under way in Croatia, where a number of places are revealing signs of ancient pans (information courtesy of Maja Grisonić). A review of the situation along the Italian side by Paola Cassola Guida (2016) has suggested various spots that potentially have Iron Age and Roman period brique-tage, among them Cupra Marittima near Ascoli Piceno where the material is argued to include votive items dedicated by the saltworkers. Sites around the Caput Adriae also continued into the Iron Age, notably the *castelliere* of Elleri.

The situation in Iberia is complex. Iberia, like Italy, has a very long coastline, so it might be expected that many other areas would have evidence of ancient *salinae*. In fact, however, none of the other likely saltworks (Cádiz, Huelva, L'Escala near Empúries/Ampurias) have produced any evidence that specific-ally indicates ancient working. Several authors have given an overview of the situation in Spain (Morère 2002; 2006; García Vargas & Martínez Maganto 2006 for the situation in general, and especially in the Cádiz area; Mangas & del Rosario Hernando 2011 for a general overview of Roman salt in Spain). Salty lagoons are present in abundance, for instance north of Cádiz near Jerez de la Frontera (Valiente Cánovas *et al.* 2017); in Aranjuez district (Lopez Gomez & Arroyo Ilera 1983); and many other areas. There are of course plenty of Roman sites in areas rich in salt: for example, the Salado river valley in Guadalajara province (Malpica Cuello *et al.* 2011), which passes the salinas of Imón and Riba de Santiuste, not far from Sigüenza, ancient Segontia; the great salinas of Añana in the Basque country, near ancient Irunia (Iruña-Veleia) in Álava province; or the series of salinas in the vicinity of ancient Astigi (Écija, Seville) (Mangas & del Rosario Hernando 2011: 66–7).

Brais Currás (2017) has considered the whole question of Roman salt pans around the Mediterranean. Apart from the coast of north-west Iberia, he lists possible salt works in the Cádiz area, at El Torrón, Huelva, as well as at Antibes in the south of France, and near Kaunos on the south-western coast of Turkey (Pliny mentions the salt of Kaunos). Few of these have produced definitive evidence of ancient salt production, however. The situation near Cádiz is interesting: there is Roman material in various places around the bay but particularly on the marshes of Roman date of San Fernando (Alonso Villalobos *et al.* 2003). What is more, a wall to contain the water in the ponds is rather similar to that found at the Maccarese lake, with stones and posts supplemented by amphorae.

The situation in Galicia and northern Portugal is different, as very significant discoveries have been made there. The most fully investigated of these is at Vigo, where the O Areal part of the city is home to the best-preserved Roman salt pans in existence (Castro Carrera 2008; Currás 2017, with references to earlier work). Here a series of enclosed ponds have been found in different parts of the shoreline, giving an estimated 8.5 ha for the full original extent of the pans. The ponds have

> a pavement of impermeable clay, on occasion compacted with gravel, and edged by schist and granite slabs [Figure 28]. The ponds are rectangular in shape and parallel, perfectly aligned with one another oriented E–W to follow the ancient coastline. The constructions vary in size and morphology. The smallest ones measure c.5 x 2.5 m, with a well-constructed flagstone pavement with a thin layer of clay. They are edged by short slabs not more than 10 cm high. (Currás 2017: 331–2)

Variations on this occur at other parts of the town. Material recovered in excavation shows that the *salina* was in use from the middle of the first century AD to the third/fourth.

Brais Currás lists and maps a considerable number of other sites in Galicia and northern Portugal, though in most cases the details and the dating are not well established.[13]

Summary

Salt was very important in the lives of people in the Greek and Roman worlds, as the ancient authors testify, and it also played an increasingly important role in the economic life of cities and the Roman state. Some scholars, indeed, attribute

---

[13] I am grateful to Brais Currás for the observation that in all these cases the sites are open to the sea, not in marshy areas (where medieval sources place saltworks), which suggests that the search for Roman saltworks has been carried out in the wrong places. He further draws my attention to the place name 'O Salnés', a district between the Pontevedra and Arousa estuaries. This toponym comes from the sixth century Parrochiale Suevum, where a 'territorium saliniense' is mentioned. There are medieval and modern salt flats along shores there, as well as saltworks that are probably Roman. Further work on Galician saltworks is in preparation: he and his collaborators have created the Mar de Sal project (Currás *et al.* forthcoming), looking at many of the Galician salt sites with a view to ensuring their preservation.

Fig. 5. East Sector (O Areal)
After César 2008, 2010, Iglesias Darriba 2009

Figure 28 Part of the excavated Roman salt pan in the East sector at Vigo, north-west Spain. Source: Currás 2017 (citing earlier reports), courtesy of Brais Currás.

Rome's rise in part to its control of the salt sources near the mouth of the river Tiber. It is not so easy, however, to show which of the many salt pans of the Mediterranean were exploited in ancient times, since the technology involved no durable artefacts and has probably changed little, so that the same pans have continued to be utilised over the centuries. Nevertheless, recent fieldwork has been able to provide important evidence for the specifics of the working methods in several cases. Continuing research in a number of areas will no doubt supplement this information in the coming years.

7 Salt as an Economic and Social Mover

Since salt was essential for human and animal health, as well as serving a range of purposes in daily life and industry, it must have had a marked effect on society and economy in the communities where it was produced and distributed. In advanced societies, particularly in states such as developed from the Roman period onwards, these effects were chronicled by historians and geographers; they are part of what constituted the ancient economy. Prior to that, the effects must also have been important, but in the absence of written records (and given that the concept of an 'economy' in those periods is inappropriate) our statements must necessarily be speculative. Nevertheless, there are many aspects for which it is possible to make reasonable assumptions.

Pliny the Elder, some of whose words on salt have already been quoted, considered salt vital to a civilised life: not only did it give food its savour, it also sharpened the wits, and enabled pleasure and relaxation. One can compare the Sermon on the Mount (Matthew 5:13), 'Ye are the salt of the earth', the origin of the famous and much-used phrase, meaning someone who is honest and worthy. Salt in traditional societies, in eastern Europe and elsewhere in the world, is given with bread as a welcome greeting ('khleb i sol' and its variants in the various Slav languages); the two substances represent what one needs for life.

The Personnel and Context of Salt Production

Who produced salt? Men or women, old or young, rich or poor? And under what circumstances? By this I refer to the social context of salt production, in other words whether it was part of a purely domestic industry in which individuals, households or groups of households took part, or an organised affair controlled from above and involving significant numbers of people engaged in specific activities.

To answer such questions, it is necessary to consider the scale of production, insofar as we can reconstruct it. In this, it is useful to work backwards in time from the Roman Imperial period. Two sources of evidence help us in this respect: the written evidence that refers to salt production sites (*salinae*) and to the individuals who worked in salt production, some of whom were called 'salinatores' (as well as the conductores discussed previously); and the evident extent of the salt pans of, for instance, Cervia and Trinitápoli. Given the suggested population of the city of Rome (at its peak probably more than one million), the scale of the requirement for salt is very evident. The *salinae romanae* near the mouth of the Tiber presumably supplied much though not all of that; thus the workforce involved must have been large (perhaps hundreds, though on modern salt pans a quite small number of workers can produce surprisingly large amounts of salt). The same applies on a smaller scale to other major cities of the Empire. It is for this reason that Giovannini suggested how important salt was to the rise of Rome; this suggests that for the last five centuries or so BC, salt production in the Roman world was a highly organised affair – though only with the rise of central authority could it be called centrally controlled.

For the Iron Age in continental Europe, things are not so straightforward. If we compare the massive production of the Seille valley with that of Atlantic and North Sea coasts, for instance, it is very clear that the former must have involved large numbers of people, the latter quite small numbers but on many sites. In all these cases where brine evaporation involved hearths or furnaces, wood was required, involving woodcutters and transporters. While the requirements of an individual Red Hill might be satisfied from its own neighbourhood, when there were dozens of such sites in an area, things cannot have been so easy; and for Marsal or Moyenvic the quantities or wood must have been significant. In this area, the scale of production can be described as proto-industrial in scale.

Farther back in time, we can distinguish between Bronze Age production involving brine boiling using briquetage, which on individual sites seems to have been very modest in scale, probably for domestic needs, and that involving much larger quantities, such as has been suggested for the trough technique in Romania. While the term 'industrial' is probably an exaggeration, it is certainly the case that the quantities of salt produced were far beyond the needs of local households, and must have been intended for trade to other communities, near or far. So an individual briquetage site required workers to hew and bring the wood, to fashion the clay containers and hearth elements, to collect the brine, and then to conduct the firing – perhaps a score or two of workers. The trough technique, on the other hand, required the felling of mature trees and the fashioning of the troughs, as well as the channelled pieces and the many other wooden elements involved; the setting up of the troughs and supplying them with fresh water; and eventually the collecting up of lumps of rock salt, processing them and distributing them across the consumer communities. It is hard to imagine this happening without several score individuals being involved.

What is more, there is one piece of evidence that indicates these tasks were not confined to males: an examination of skeletal remains from graves at Hallstatt showed that females had strong muscle attachments associated with hard physical work (Pany & Teschler-Nicola 2007). Such women were not, it seems, aristocrats whose control of the salt source enabled them to sit back and watch others do the work. In other areas, some of the tasks involved required physical strength that is usually associated with men, such as tree-felling and carpentry. Other tasks, such as the fashioning of clay containers or furnace elements could have been carried out by males or females. The consequence is that salt production was probably carried out by all members of a community, male and female, young and old (one may recall that the adits in many copper mines are so narrow that only children could have managed to get into them).

Effects of Wealth in Salt

It has become a cliché that control of the salt sources of Iron Age Europe enabled wealth and prestige for those involved. Nowhere has this been more repeated than in the case of Hallstatt. Many of the graves in the cemetery that lies on the plateau beside the mining areas are well provisioned with goods, typically weapons (swords and daggers) but also decorative items for personal adornment. The question arises, how did people buried some 350 m up a mountainside acquire such 'wealth'? If it was control of the salt trade, how did such a process work? There are several places in the Early Iron Age world that are much 'richer' than Hallstatt, and which have no known connection with salt – the famous graves at Hochdorf or the Hohmichele/Heuneburg area in Baden-Württemberg, for instance. What is more, the salt mines at Hallstatt were, as we have seen, very active in the Bronze Age without any indication of special treatment of the dead in the area.

Were salt workers special people? The appearance of briquetage in graves, discussed by Jockenhovel (2012), suggests that there was a special role in society assigned to salt workers, something that stayed with them even after death. Indeed, salt workers may have possessed something of the mysterious quality of smiths, often encountered in pre-industrial societies, past and present. Metalsmiths produced a new material out of lumps of rock; salt workers produced a new material out of water. While this may not be sufficient to explain why people at Hallstatt were specially provisioned in death, it does suggest that there was a special place in society reserved for such people.

Salt has also been seen to have an almost magical quality. A Spanish group, who have worked on prehistoric salt production in the Vilafáfila area north of Zamora, point to the presence of pits in the production area full of animal bones, carbonised grain, pottery and stones as evidence for a range of ritual activities (Abarquero Moras *et al.* 2012). The salt in the Ourania cave in Crete has been suggested to have had a ritual significance. The requirement for salted meal (*mola salsa*) in Roman ritual also suggests a connection between ritual obser-vance and salted products.

In the absence of specific information about how the processes of salt production and distribution worked, it is not possible to be more specific about the way in which individuals or communities might have capitalised on the presence of their resource. In any event, a straightforward correlation between wealth and salt availability cannot be sustained.

Processes: Production, Transport and Distribution

In previous sections, I have described what is known of the various processes by which salt was produced. This is a technical matter and takes no account of the ways by which the human actors exercised their mental processes to guide motor actions, in other words the relationship between intention and execution. This process is often called the *chaîne opératoire*, though there is no reason why English speakers should not refer to the 'production sequence' or something similar. In a previous work (Harding 2013), I have endeavoured to set out the steps involved in such a sequence, from identifying brine springs, procuring wood or charcoal, creating clay forms and containers or fashioning wooden elements, conducting the evaporation or quarrying process, and collecting up the resultant crystals or lumps. Obviously the details will differ in each of the processes involved. What is important is to recognise the way in which salt workers followed a set of steps in a logical sequence to create the desired result. The way in which people learn the necessary motor skills to perform a task has been much examined in recent years, and applies to salt as much as to other skills such as potting (e.g. Manem 2020).

A useful diagram of the processes involved in turning sea salt into a form that could be used by ancient communities is provided by Sevink (2020) (Figure 29).

Once salt had been turned into a usable form, if it was intended for supplying distant communities it had to be put into containers and transported. In the case of briquetage, it appears that crystalline salt was moved in the brine containers themselves after evaporation: there appears to be no other explanation for its regular appearance on sites far from the coast or the brine sources. How this was achieved is not known; presumably pack animals were used, using panniers with straw protecting the clay vessels. The same might apply to salt obtained from mines or outcrops, dissolved and turned into crystalline form after evaporation. Salt in this form can be compressed into blocks and transported on pack animals, using cord and nets to keep it in place (as is seen in historical and modern salt transport in Saharan Africa).

Riverine transport is well known in historical times in central and eastern Europe (e.g. Marc 2006); Valeriu Cavruc and I attempted to chart the possible

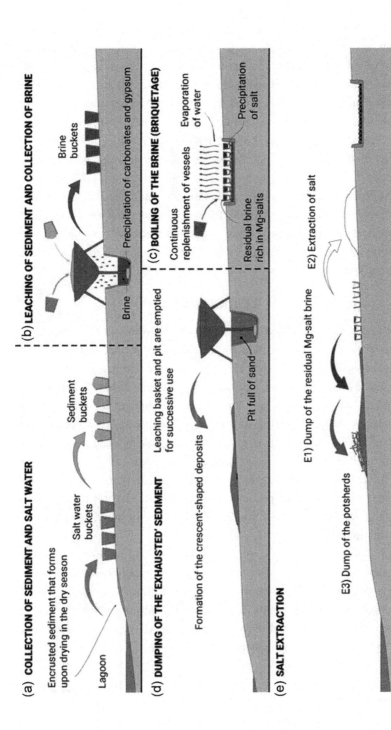

Figure 29 Reconstruction of the production sequence at Puntone, Tuscany. Source: Sevink *et al.* 2020 courtesy of Jan Sevink.

ways in which Carpathian and Transylvanian salt might have moved in ancient times (Harding & Kavruk 2013: 212ff.). The output of major sources such as Hallstatt, the Halle area or the Seille valley, is very likely to have used the major rivers for distribution across their consumer areas, as well as land transport. Mangas and del Rosario Hernando (2011: 73ff.) have considered the same matter, both for Spain and for the wider Mediterranean, including mention of an inscription from a statue base found near Ostia referring to the 'sack-carriers' (i.e. transporters) of the city and the saltworks. In this case, the transport obviously went along the Roman road system, including the *via salaria*.[14]

In the Roman and medieval periods, salt stores and depots are known to have developed: such was the case for the legionary fortress of Apulum, for instance. Although such evidence is not securely attested for the prehistoric period, it is possible that major late Iron Age sites served similar purposes.

8 Conclusion

People in ancient times liked and valued salt and went out of their way to procure it. From the Bronze Age on, and possibly earlier, salt production became an established industry. Even if the quantities that modern medicine specifies as essential for healthy life are higher than what people in saltless regions can survive on, nonetheless the 'hunger for salt' that has been described by anthropologists and animal health experts indicates how important the substance is. It is not correct to speak of an 'economy' until detailed written records give us usable information (as for Greece and Rome in the later Iron Age and Imperial period), but it is clear that significant numbers of people and resources must have been devoted to salt production. This in itself would have had a corresponding impact on social relations.

For modern western people, for whom salt involves no more than a trip to the supermarket, it is hard to imagine its role in pre-industrial societies, or the processes by which it arrives on our tables. Whereas the highly mechanised form of production seen in modern salt mines supplies all the salt needed for industry, and much of what is eaten, there are still artisanal forms of production, for instance the *fleur de sel* coming from the

---

[14] *genio saccariorum salarior[um] totius urbis camp[i] sal[inarum] rom[anorum]* ... (*CIL* XIV 4285), found in the *stagnum portuense* at the locality named *campo saline*. On the reverse is an image of a boat with sacks being carried on.

Guérande salt marshes in the Pradel area of western France, that supply specialist outlets and which connoisseurs regard as superior in flavour. In similar fashion, Pliny regarded some types of salt as superior to others. Societies and economies may change, but humans need salt, wherever and whenever they lived and live.

Bibliography

Abarquero Moras, F. J. & Guerra Doce, E. (eds.) (2010). *Los yacimientos de Villafáfila (Zamora) en el marco de las explotaciones salineras de la prehistoria europea*. Valladolid: Junta de Castilla y León, Consejería de Cultura y Turismo.

Abarquero Moras, F. J. *et al.* (2010). Excavaciones en los 'cocederos' de sal prehistóricos de Molino Sanchón II y Santioste (Villafáfila, Zamora). In F. J. Abarquero Moras and E. Guerra Doce (eds.), *Los yacimientos de Villafáfila (Zamora) en el marco de las explotaciones salineras de la prehistoria europea*, pp. 85–118. Valladolid: Junta de Castilla y León, Consejería de Cultura y Turismo.

Abarquero Moras, F. J. *et al.* (2012). *Arqueología de la Sal en las Lagunas de Villafáfila (Zamora): Investigaciones sobre los cocederos prehistóricos*. Valladolid: Junta Castilla y León. Arqueología en Castilla y León, Monografías 9.

Abdel-Aal, H., Zohdy, K. & Abdelkreem, M. (2017). Seawater bittern a precursor for magnesium chloride separation: discussion and assessment of case studies, *International Journal of Waste Resources* 7(1), http://doi.org/10.4172/2252–5211.1000267.

Adshead, S. A. M. (1992). *Salt and Civilisation*. Basingstoke & London: Macmillan.

Alessandri, L. *et al.* (2019). Salt or fish (or salted fish)? The Bronze Age specialised sites along the Tyrrhenian coast of Central Italy: new insights from Caprolace settlement, *PLOS ONE* 14(11), e0224435, https://doi.org/10.1371/journal.pone.0224435.

Alonso Villalobos, C., Gracia Prieto, F. J. & Ménanteau, L. (2003). Las salinas de la bahía de Cádiz durante la Antigüedad: visión geoarqueológica de un problema histórico, *SPAL Revista de Prehistoria y Arqueología de la Universidad de Sevilla* 12, 317–32.

Andronic, M. (1989). Cacica – un nou punct neolitic de exploatare a sării, *Studii şi cercetări de istorie veche şi arheologie* 40(2), 171–7.

Ard, V. & Weller, O. (2012). Les vases de 'type Champ-Durand': témoins d'une exploitation du sel au Néolithique récent dans le Marais poitevin. In R. Joussaume (ed.), *L'enceinte néolithique de Champ-Durand à Nieul-sur-6 l'Autise (Vendée)*, pp. 319–43. Chauvigny: Association des Publications Chauvinoises.

Arrowsmith, P. & Power, D. (eds.) (2012). *Roman Nantwich: A Salt-making settlement. Excavations at Kingsley Fields 2002*. BAR British series 557. Oxford: Archaeopress.

Bánffy, E. (2015). The beginnings of salt exploitation in the Carpathian Basin (6th–5th millennium BC), *Documenta Praehistorica* 42, 197–209.

Barth, F. E. (1990). *Salzbergwerk Hallstatt: Kernverwässerungswerk Grabung 1849*. Hallstatt: Musealverein Hallstatt.

Barth, F. E., Felber, H. & Schauberger, O. (1975). Radiokohlenstoffdatierung der prähistorischen Baue in den Salzbergwerken Hallstatt und Dürrnberg-Hallein, *Mitteilungen der anthropologischen Gesellschaft in Wien* 105, 45–52.

Bednarczyk, J. *et al.* (2015). Ancient salt exploitation in the Polish lowlands: recent research and future perspectives. In R. Brigand and O. Weller (eds.), *Archaeology of Salt: Approaching an invisible past*, pp. 103–24. Leiden: Sidestone.

Bell, A., Gurney, D. & Healey, H. (1999). *Lincolnshire Salterns: Excavations at Helpringham, Holbeach St Johns and Bicker Haven*. Heckington (Sleaford): Heritage Trust of Lincolnshire. East Anglian Archaeology, Report 89.

Bell, M. (1990). *Brean Down Excavations 1983–1987*. London: English Heritage. English Heritage Archaeological Report 15.

Benac, A. (1978). Neke karakteristike neolitskih naselja u Bosni i Hercegnovi, *Materijali X. kongresa arheologa Jugoslavije (Prilep 1976)* 14, 15–26.

Bérard, G. & Barruol, G. (1997). *Carte archéologique de la Gaule romaine, 4. Les Alpes-de-Haute-Provence*. Paris: Les Editions de la MSH.

Bergier, J.-F. (1982). *Une histoire du sel*. Fribourg: Office du Livre.

Bestwick, J.D. (1975). Romano-British inland salting at Middlewich (Salinae). In K. W. De Brisay and K. A. Evans (eds.), *Salt: The study of an ancient industry*, pp. 66–70. Colchester: Colchester Archaeological Group.

Biddulph, E. (2013). Salt of the earth: Roman industry at Stanford Wharf, *Current Archaeology* 276, 16–22.

Biddulph, E. *et al.* (2012). *London Gateway: Iron Age and Roman salt making in the Thames Estuary. Excavation at Stanford Wharf Nature Reserve, Essex*. Oxford: Oxford Archaeology. Oxford Archaeology Monograph 18.

Bönisch, E. (1993). Briquetage aus bronzezeitlichen Gräbern der Niederlausitz, *Arbeits- und Forschungsberichte zur sächsischen Bodendenkmalpflege* 36, 67–84.

Borrell, F., Boscha, J. & Majó, T. (2015). Life and death in the Neolithic variscite mines at Gavà (Barcelona, Spain), *Antiquity* 89, 72–90.

Brothwell, D. R. & Brothwell, P. (1969). *Food in Antiquity: A survey of the diet of early peoples*. London: Thames & Hudson. Ancient Peoples and Places, 66.

Brown, I. W. (1981). *The Role of Salt in Eastern North American Prehistory*. Baton Rouge, LA: Department of Culture, Recreation and Tourism, & Louisiana Archaeological Survey and Antiquities Commission.

Bukowski, Z. (1985). Salt production in Poland in prehistoric times, *Archaeologia Polona* 24, 27–71.

Buzea, D. L. (2010). Experimentul 'Troaca', *Angustia* 14, 245–56.

Buzea, D. L. (2013). The exploitation of rock salt using wooden troughs: experiments conducted at Băile Figa in 2008–2010. In A. Harding and V. Kavruk (eds.), *Explorations in Salt Archaeology in the Carpathian Zone*, pp. 185–92. Budapest: Archaeolingua.

Buzea, D. L. (2018). Raport preliminar asupra experimentelor arheologice desfășurate la Beclean – Băile Figa jud. Bistrița-Năsăud, 2017 – 2018. Utilizarea 'troacelor' și instalațiilor din lemn în procesul de extragere și exploatare a surselor de sare, slatină și nămol sărat (I) / Preliminary report on the archaeological experiments in Beclean – Băile Figa, Bistrița-Năsăud county, 2017–2018. The use of troughs and wooden installations for the saline resources, brine and salty mud extraction and exploitation (I), *Angustia* 22, 9–135.

Cabal, M. & Thoen, H. (1985). L'industrie du sel à Ardres à l'époque romaine, *Revue du Nord* 67(264), 193–206, https://doi.org/10.3406/rnord .1985.4098.

Carpentier, V. & Marcigny, C. (2019). Apports de l'archéologie à la connaissance des économies salicoles sur les côtes de la Manche (Protohistoire-époque moderne). In C. Chauveau (ed.), *Les archéologues face à l'économie*, pp. 140–7. Paris: Inrap / Éditions Faton. Archéopages: archéologie & société, Hors série 5.

Carpentier, V., Ghesquière, E. & Marcigny, C. (2012). *Grains de Sel. Itinéraire dans les salines du littoral bas-normand de la préhistoire au XIXe siècle*. Bayeux: Orep Éditions (revised edition; first edition published 2006 by Centre Régional d'Archéologie d'Alet and Association Manche Atlantique pour la Recherche Archéologique dans les Îles).

Carusi, C. (2006). Essai d'histoire du sel dans le monde grec. In J.-C. Hocquet and J.-L. Sarrazin (eds.), *Le sel de la Baie: histoire, archéologie, ethnologie des sels atlantiques*, pp. 55–63. Rennes: Presses universitaires de Rennes.

Carusi, C. (2008). *Il sale nel mondo greco (VI a.C.-III d.C.): Luoghi di produzione, circolazione commerciale, regimi di sfruttamento nel contesto del Mediterraneo antico*. Bari: Edipuglia. Pragmateiai.

Carusi, C. (2015). 'VITA HUMANIOR SINE SALE QUIT DEGERE': Demand for salt and salt trade patterns in the ancient Greek world. In E. M. Harris, D. M. Lewis and M. Woolmer (eds.), *The Ancient Greek Economy:*

Markets, households and city-states, pp.337–55. Cambridge: Cambridge University Press.

Carusi, C. (2018). Salt and fish processing in the ancient Mediterranean: a brief survey, *Journal of Maritime Archaeology* 13, 481–90.

Cassen, S., Labriffe, P.-A. & Ménanteau, L. (2006). Le sel «chauffé» des baies marines en Armorique-Sud durant les Ve et IVe millénaire av. J.-C.: à la recherche (Ouest-européenne) de croyances et de faits techniques. In J.-C. Hocquet and J.-L. Sarrazin (eds.), *Le sel de la Baie: histoire, archéologie, ethnologie des sels atlantiques*, pp. 33–54. Rennes: Presses universitaires de Rennes.

Cassen, S., Labriffe, P.-A. & Ménanteau, L. (2008). Washing and heating on the Neolithic shores of western Europe: an archaeological hypothesis on the production of sea salt. In O. Weller, A. Dufraisse and P. Pétrequin (eds.), *Sel, eau et forêt, d'hier à aujourd'hui*, pp. 175–204. Besançon: Presses universitaires de Franche-Comté.

Cassola Guida, P. & Montagnari Kokelj, E. (2006). Produzione di sale nel golfo di Trieste: un'attività probabilmente antica. In *Studi di protostoria in onore di Renato Peroni*, pp. 327–32. Firenze: All'Insegna del Giglio.

Cassola Guida, P. (2016). Il sale nella protostoria dell'Adriatico: una proposta di interpretazione per il deposito votivo di Cupra Marittima (Ascoli Piceno), *West & East* 1, 38–63.

Castro Carrera, J. C. (2008). La saline romaine de «O Areal», Vigo (Galice): architecture d'une installation industrielle de production de sel marin. In O. Weller, A. Dufraisse and P. Pétrequin (eds.), *Sel, eau et forêt, d'hier à aujourd'hui*, pp. 381–99. Besançon: Presses universitaires de Franche-Comté.

Cébeillac-Gervasoni, M. & Morelli, C. (2014). Les *conductores* du *Campus Salinarum Romanarum*, *Mélanges de l'École française de Rome* 126–1, https://doi.org/10.4000/mefra.2075.

Chowne, P. *et al.* (2001). *Excavations at Billingborough, Lincolnshire, 1975–8: A Bronze-Iron Age settlement and salt-working site*. Salisbury: Wessex Archaeology. East Anglian Archaeology Report 94.

Crowson, A. (2001). Excavation of a Late Roman saltern at Blackborough End, Middleton, Norfolk. In T. Lane and E. L. Morris (eds.), *A Millennium of Saltmaking: Prehistoric and Roman-British salt production in the Fenland*, pp. 162–249. Sleaford: Heritage Trust of Lincolnshire. Lincolnshire Archaeology and Heritage Reports Series, 4.

Currás, B. X. (2017). The salinae of O Areal (Vigo) and Roman salt production in NW Iberia, *Journal of Roman Archaeology* 30, 325–49.

Currás, B. X. *et al.* (forthcoming). Roman salt production in Northwest Iberia and heritage management: The Mar de Sal project, *Antiquity* Project Gallery.

Daire, M.-Y. (2003). *Le sel des Gaulois*. Paris: éditions errance. Collection des Hesperides.

Daire, M.-Y. (ed.) (1994). *Le sel gaulois. Bouilleurs de sel et ateliers de briquetages armoricains à l'Âge du Fer*. Saint-Malo: Les Dossiers du Centre Régional d'Archéologie d'Alet, supplement Q.

Dębiec, M. & Saile, T. (2018). Praveké varenie soli v údolí rieky Tyrawka v Górach Słonnych / Prehistoric salt-making in the valley of the Tyrawka River in the Słonne Mountains. In M. Javor, S. Jędrzejewska and J. Ligoda (eds.), *Wspólne dziedzictwo pogranicze słowacko-polskie w epoce brązu / Common heritage the Slovakian-Polish borderland in the Bronze Age*, pp. 135–41. Rzeszów: Oficyna wydawnicza Zimowit.

Dębiec, M., Posselt, M. & Saile, T. (2015). Tyrawa Solna. Salz, Siedlungen und eine Magnetometerprospektion an der Tyrawka in den Salzbergen der Beskiden, *Spawozdania Archeologiczne* 67, 189–97.

Denton, D. A. (1984). *The Hunger for Salt: An anthropological, physiological and medical analysis*. Berlin; Heidelberg; New York; Tokyo: Springer-Verlag.

Desfossés, Y. (ed.) (2000). *Archéologie préventive en Vallée de Canche. Les sites protohistoriques fouillés dans le cadre de la réalisation de l'Autoroute A.16*. Nord-Ouest Archéologie 11. Berck-sur-Mer: Centre de Recherches Archéologiques et de Diffusion Culturelle.

Di Fraia, T. & Secoli, L. (2002). Il sito dell'età del bronzo di Isola di Coltano. In N. Negroni Catacchio (ed.), *Atti Quinto Incontro di Studi di Preistoria e Protostoria in Etruria 'Paesaggi d'acque'*, pp. 79–93. Milan: Centro Studi di Preistoria e Archeologia.

Di Fraia, T. (2011). Salt production and consumption in prehistory: toward a complex systems view. In A. Vianello (ed.), *Exotica in the Prehistoric Mediterranean*, pp. 26–32. Oxford: Oxbow Books.

Diaconu, V. (2018). Prezenţa unor recipiente de lut legate de exploatarea sării în aşezări ale culturii Cucuteni de la răsărit de Carpaţi, *Arheologia Moldovei* 41, 179–92.

Dumas, A. A. & Eubanks, P. N. (eds.) 2021. *Salt in Eastern North America and the Caribbean: History and archaeology*. Tuscaloosa: University of Alabama Press.

Dumitroaia, G. *et al.* (2008). Un nou punct de exploatare a apei sărate în preistorie: Ţolici-Hălăbutoaia, jud. Neamţ. In D. Monah, G. Dumitroaia and D. Garvăn (eds.), *Sarea, de la Prezent la Trecut*, pp. 203–24. Piatra Neamţ: Editura Constantin Matasă. Bibliotheca Memoriae Antiquitatis, XX.

Escacena Carrasco, J. L. & Garcia Rivero, D. (2019). Producción neolítica de sal marina en la Marismilla (la Puebla del Río, Sevilla). Datos renovados e hipótesis complementarias, *LVCENTVM* 38, 9–26.

Ettel, P., Ipach, S. & Schneider, F. (2018). *Salz in Mitteldeutschland: Salzsieder-Siedlungen der Bronze- und Eisenzeit*. Jena: Friedrich-Schiller-Universität Jena. Jenaer Archäologische Forschungen 4.

Farrar, R. A. H. (1975). Prehistoric and Roman saltworks in Dorset. In K. W. De Brisay and K. A. Evans (eds.), *Salt: The study of an ancient industry*, pp. 14–20. Colchester: Colchester Archaeological Group.

Fawn, A. J. *et al.* (eds.) (1990). *The Red Hills of Essex: Salt-making in Antiquity*. Colchester: Colchester Archaeological Group.

Fell, D. W. (2020). *Contact, Concord and Conquest: Britons and Romans at Scotch Corner*. Barnard Castle: Northern Archaeological Associates. NAA Monograph Series Volume 5.

Figuls, A. *et al.* (2007). Neolithic exploitation of halite at the 'Val Salina' of Cardona (Catalonia, Spain). In A. Figuls and O. Weller (eds.), *1a Trobada internacional d'arqueologia envers l'explotatió de la sal a la prehistòria i protohistòria, Cardona, 6–8 de desembre del 2003*, pp. 199–218. Cardona: Institut de recerques envers la Cultura (IREC). Archaeologia Cardonensis 1.

Fíguls, A. *et al.* (2013). La primera explotacion minera de la sal gema: la Vall Salina de Cardona (Cataluña, España), *Chungara, Revista de Antropología Chilena* 45, 177–95.

Flad, R. (2011). *Salt Production and Social Hierarchy in Ancient China: An archaeological investigation of specialization in China's Three Gorges*. New York: Cambridge University Press.

Forenbaher, S. (2013). Pretpovijesni tragovi proizvodnje soli u podvelebitskom primorju, *Senjski zbornik* 40, 179–94.

Fraś, J. M. (2001). Zarys osadnictwa neolitycznego na terenie Wieliczki i okolicy, *Studia i materiały do dziejów żup solnych w Polsce* 21, 283–319.

García Vargas, E. & Maganto, J. M. (2017). Salines d'évaporation solaire dans l'Empire romain: témoignages archéologiques d'une activité éphémère. In R. González Villaescusa, K. Schörle, F. Gayet and F. Rechin (eds.), *L'exploitation des ressources maritimes de l'Antiquité: Activités productives et organisation des territoires. Actes des Rencontres 11–13 octobre 2016*, pp. 197–212. Antibes: Éditions APDCA.

García Vargas, E. & Martínez Maganto, J. (2006). La sal de la Bética romana. Algunas cuestiones sobre su explotación y comercio, *HABIS* 253–74.

Gauci, R., Schembri, J. A. & Inkpen, R. (2017). Traditional use of shore platforms: a study of the artisanal management of salinas on the Maltese islands (central Mediterranean), *SAGE Open* April–June 2017, 1–16. https://DOI.org/10.1177/2158244017706597.

Giot, P.-R., L'Helgouach, J. & Briard, J. (1965). Le site du Curnic en Guisseny, *Annales de Bretagne* 72, 49–70.

Giovannini, A. (1985). Le sel et la fortune de Rome, *Athenaeum* 63, 373–87.

Giovannini, A. (2001). Les salines d'Ostie. In J.-P. Descœudres (ed.), *Ostia, port et porte de la Rome antique*, pp. 36–8. Geneva: Musée Rath, Genève.

Godelier, M. (1969). La « monnaie de sel » des Baruya de Nouvelle-Guinée, *L'Homme* 9/2, 5–37.

Good, C. (1995). Salt production and commerce in Guerrero, Mexico: an ethnographic contribution to historical reconstruction, *Ancient Mesoamerica* 6, 1–13.

Gouletquer, P. L. & Kleinmann, D. (1984). Les salines du Manga (Niger). In C. Lefébure and P. Lemonnier (eds.), *'Des choses dont la recherche est laborieuse . . .'*, pp. Paris: Maison des sciences de l'Homme. Techniques et Cultures. Bulletin de l'Equipe de Recherche 191, 3. https://doi.org/10.4000/tc.998.

Gouletquer, P. L. & Weller, O. (2002). Y a-t-il eu des salines au néolithique en Bretagne? In F. Péron (ed.), *Le patrimoine maritime. Construire, transmettre, utiliser, symboliser les héritages maritimes européens*, pp. 449–53. Rennes: Presses Universitaires Rennes.

Gouletquer, P. L. (1969). Etudes sur les briquetages, IV, *Annales de Bretagne* 76, 119–47.

Gouletquer, P. L. (1970). *Les briquetages armoricains. Technologie protohistorique du sel en Armorique*. Rennes: Travaux du Laboratoire d'Anthropologie Préhistorique, Faculté des Sciences.

Gouletquer, P. L. (1975). Niger, country of salt. In K. W. De Brisay and K. A. Evans (eds.), *Salt: The Study of an Ancient Industry*, pp. 47–51. Colchester: Colchester Archaeological Group.

Grabner, M. *et al.* (2006). Dendrochronologie in Hallstatt, *Archäologie Österreichs* 17(1), 40–9.

Grabner, M. *et al.* (2007). Bronze age dating of timber from the salt-mine at Hallstatt, Austria, *Dendrochronologia* 24, 61–8.

Grabowska, M. (1967). Badania wykopaliskowe w Baryczy-Krzyszkowicach, pow. Kraków, na stanowisku VII, *Badania archeologiczne prowadzone przez Muzeum Żup Krakowskich Wieliczka w roku 1967*, 13–17.

Grossi, M.C. *et al.* (2015). A complex relationship between human and natural landscape: a multidisciplinary approach to the study of the roman saltworks in 'Le Vignole-Interporto' (Maccarese, Fiumicino-Roma). In R. Brigand and O. Weller (eds.), *Archaeology of Salt: Approaching an invisible past*, pp. 83–101. Leiden: Sidestone.

Grove, J. & Brunning, R. (1998). The Romano-British salt industry in Somerset, *Archaeology in the Severn Estuary* 9, 61–8.

Guerra Doce, E. (2016). Salt and Beakers in the third millennium BC. In E. Guerra Doce and C. L. v. Lettow-Vorbeck (eds.), *Analysis of the Economic Foundations Supporting the Social Supremacy of the Beaker Groups. Proceedings of the XVII UISPP World Congress (1–7 September, Burgos, Spain)*. Vol. 6 / Session B36, pp. 95–110. Oxford: Archaeopress.

Guerra Doce, E. (2017). La sal y el campaniforme en la península Ibérica: fuente de riqueza, instrumento de poder ¿y detonante del origen del estilo marítimo? In V. S. Gonçalves (ed.), *Sinos e Taças. Junto ao oceano e mais longe. Aspectos da presença campaniforme na península Ibérica*, pp. 342–53. Lisbon: Centro de Arqueologia da Universidade de Lisboa / Faculdade de Letras da Universidade de Lisboa. estudos & memórias 10.

Guerra Doce, E. *et al.* (2011). The Beaker salt production centre of Molino Sanchón II, Zamora, Spain, *Antiquity* 85,

Hamon, C. (2016). Salt mining tools and techniques from Duzdaği (Nakhchivan, Azerbaijan) in the 5th to 3rd millennium B.C., *Journal of Field Archaeology* 41(4), 510–28.

Hannois, P. (1999). Répertoire céramique ménapien et données nouvelles sur la fabrication du sel, *Revue du Nord* 81(333) Archéologie de la Picardie et du Nord de la France, 107–19.

Hansen, L. (2016). *Die latènezeitliche Saline von Bad Nauheim. Die Befunde der Grabungen der Jahre 2001–2004 in der Kurstraße 2.* Wiesbaden: Landesamt für Denkmalpflege Hessen. Fundberichte aus Hessen, Beiheft 8.

Harding, A. & Kavruk, V. (2013). *Explorations in Salt Archaeology in the Carpathian Zone.* Budapest: Archaeolingua.

Harding, A. (2013). *Salt in Prehistoric Europe.* Leiden: Sidestone Press.

Hocquet, J.-C. (1978–79). *Le sel et la fortune de Venise*, vols. 1–2. Lille: Presses Universitaires.

Hocquet, J.-C. (1986). L'évolution des techniques de fabrication du sel marin sur les rivages de l'Europe du Nord-Ouest (position des problèmes), *Revue du Nord* 1 spécial hors série, 3–22.

Hocquet, J.-C. (1991). *Chioggia, capitale del sale nel Medioevo.* Chioggia: Libreria Editrice.

Hocquet, J.-C. (1994). Production et commerce du sel à l'Age du Fer et à l'époque romaine dans l'Europe du Nord-Ouest, *Revue du Nord* 76(308), 9–20.

Hocquet, J.-C. (2001). *Hommes et Paysages du Sel. Une aventure millénaire.* Arles: Actes Sud.

Hocquet, J.-C. (2019). *Le sel. De l'esclavage à la mondialisation.* Paris: CNRS Éditions.

Hughes, S., Naomi, P. & Rainbird, P. (2017). Salt of the hearth: understanding the briquetage from a later Romano-British saltern at Pyde Drove, near Woolavington, Somerset, *Britannia* 48, 117–133.

Huijzendveld, A. (n.d.). The historical salt works of the coastal plain of Rome, www.ostia-foundation.org/the-historical-salt-works-of-the-coastal-plain-of-rome/, accessed 20 December 2020.

Hurst, J. D. (ed.) (1997). *A Multi-period Salt Production Site at Droitwich: Excavations at Upwich*. CBA Research Report 107. York: Council for British Archaeology.

Hurst, J. D. (ed.) (2006). *Roman Droitwich: Dodderhill fort, Bays Meadow villa, and roadside settlement*. CBA Research Report 146. York: Council for British Archaeology.

Ipach, S. (2016). *Die Salzsieder-Fundplätze der älteren Eisenzeit von Erdeborn in Sachsen-Anhalt und Steinthaleben in Thüringen*. Jena, Langenweissbach: Beier & Beran. Jenaer Schriften zur Vor- und Frühgeschichte 6.

Jockenhövel, A. (2012). Bronzezeitliche Sole in Mitteldeutschland: Gewinnung – Distribution – Symbolik. In V. Nikolov and K. Bacvarov (eds.), *Salt and Gold: The role of salt in prehistoric Europe*, pp. 239–57. Provadia / Veliko Tarnovo: Verlag Faber.

Jodłowski, A. (1968). Badania urządzeń solankowych kultury lendzelskiej w Baryczy, pow. Kraków, *Badania archeologiczne prowadzone przez Muzeum Żup Krakowskich Wieliczka w roku 1968*, 13–20.

Jodłowski, A. (1971). *Eksploatacja sóli na terenie Małopolski w pradziejach i we wczesnym średniowieczu*. Wieliczka: Muzeum Żup Krakowskich. Studia i materiały do dziejów żup sólnych w Polsce, 4.

Jodłowski, A. (1977). Die Salzgewinnung auf polnischen Boden in vor-geschichtlicher Zeit und im frühen Mittelalter, *Jahresschrift fur Mitteldeutsche Vorgeschichte* 61, 85–103.

Jones, A. K. G. (1983). A coprolite from 6 – 8 Pavement. In A. R. Hall, H. K. Kenward, D. Williams and J. R. A. Greig (eds.), *Environment and Living Conditions at Two Anglo-Scandinavian Sites*, pp. 225–9. York: Council for British Archaeology. The Archaeology of York, Vol 14: The Past Environment of York, Fascicule 4.

Kadrow, S. & Nowak-Włodarczak, E. (2003). Osada kultury łużyckiej na stan. 27 w Krakowie-Bieżanowie – organizacja warzelnictwa soli. In J. Gancarski (ed.), *Epoka brązu i wczesna epoka żelaza w Karpatach polskich*, pp. 549–67. Krosno: Muzeum Podkarpackie w Krośnie.

Kadrow, S. (2003). Charakterystyka technologiczna ceramiki kultury łużyckiej. In S. Kadrow (ed.), *Kraków-Bieżanów, stanowisko 27 i Kraków-Rząka, sta-nowisko 1, osada kultury łużyckiej*, pp. 205–20. Kraków: Zespół do Badań

Autostrad. Via Archaeologica. Źródła z badań wykopaliskowych na trasie autostrady A4 w Małopolsce.

Kerger, P. (1999). Etude du matériel archéologique de l'atelier de sauniers à De Panne (Fl.-Occ.), *Lunula* 7, 74–81.

Kern, A. *et al.* (eds.) (2009). *Kingdom of Salt: 7000 years of Hallstatt* (English version of *Salz-Reich. 7000 Jahre Hallstatt*, 2008). Veröffentlichungen der prähistorischen Abteilung 3. Vienna:Naturhistorisches Museum.

Kinory, J. (2012). *Salt Production, Distribution and Use in the British Iron Age.* Oxford: Archaeopress. BAR British Series 559.

Kopaka, K. & Chaniotakis, N. (2003). Just taste additive? Bronze Age salt from Zakros, Crete, *Oxford Journal of Archaeology* 22/1, 53–66.

Kull, B. (ed.) (2003). *Sole und Salz schreiben Geschichte. 50 Jahre Landesarchäologie: 150 Jahre Archäologische Forschung in Bad Nauheim.* Archäologische und Paläontologische Denkmalpflege, Landesamt für Denkmalpflege Hessen. Mainz: von Zabern.

Kurlansky, M. (2002). *Salt: A World History.* London: Jonathan Cape.

Lane, T. & Morris, E. L. (eds.) (2001). *A Millennium of Saltmaking: Prehistoric and Romano-British salt production in the Fenland.* Sleaford: Heritage Trust of Lincolnshire. Lincolnshire Archaeology and Heritage Reports Series, 4.

Lane, T. (2018). *Mineral from the Marshes: Coastal salt-making in Lincolnshire.* Sleaford: Heritage Trust of Lincolnshire. Lincolnshire Archaeology and Heritage Reports Series, 12.

Lane, T., Hogan, S. & Robinson Zeki, L. (2019). Excavations of salterns at Fenland Way, Chatteris and Camel Road, Littleport, Cambridgeshire, *Proceedings of the Cambridge Antiquarian Society* 108, 51–72.

Laumann, H. (2000). Hallstattzeitliche Salzsiederei in Werl. In H. G. Horn, H. Hellenkemper, G. Isenberg and H. Koschik (eds.), *Millionen Jahre Geschichte, Fundort Nordrhein-Westfalen. Begleitbuch zur Landesausstellung*, pp. 250–1. Mainz: von Zabern.

Lazarovici, G. & Lazarovici, C.-M. (2011). Some salt sources in Transylvania and their connections with the archaeological sites in the area. In M. Alexianu, O. Weller and R.-G. Curca (eds.), *Archaeology and Anthropology of Salt. Proceedings of the International Colloquium, 1–5 October 2008. Al. I. Cuza University (Iaşi, Romania)*, pp. 89–110. Oxford: Archaeopress. British Archaeological Reports, International Series 2198.

Leech, R. H. (1977). Late Iron Age and Romano-British briquetage sites at Quarrylands Lane, Badgworth, *Somerset Archaeology and Natural History* 121, 89–96.

Leech, R. H. (1981). The Somerset Levels in the Romano-British period. In T. Rowley (ed.), *The Evolution of Marshland Landscapes: Papers presented to a conference on marshland landscapes held in Oxford in December 1979*, pp. 20–51. Oxford: Oxford University, Department for External Studies.

Leidinger, W. (1996). Salzgewinnung an den Solquellen der Saline Werl. In R. Just and U. Meissner (eds.), *Das Leben in der Saline – Arbeiter und Unternehmer*, pp. 189–215. Halle/Saale: Technisches Halloren- und Salinemuseum. Schriften und Quellen zur Kulturgeschichte des Salzes 3 (also separately published as a pamphlet, 27 pp.).

Liot, C. (2002). «Briquetages» et production de sels par lessivage de terres salées au Mexique. In O. Weller (ed.), *Archéologie du sel: techniques et sociétés dals al Pré- et Protohistoire européenne / Salzarchäologie: Techniken und Gesellschaft in der Vor- und Frühgeschichte Europas*, pp. 81–98. Rahden/Westf.: Marie Leidorf.

Lopez Gomez, A. & Arroyo Ilera, F. (1983). Antiguas salinas de la comarca de Aranjuez, *Estudios Geográficos* 44(172), 339–71.

Lovejoy, P. E. (1986). *Salt and the Desert Sun: A history of salt production and trade in Central Sudan*. Cambridge: Cambridge University Press.

Malpica Cuello, A. *et al.* (2011). Paisajes de la sal en la Meseta castellana desde la Prehistoria a la Edad Media: el valle del Salado (Guadalajara). In M. Jiménez Puertas and G. García-Contreras Ruiz (eds.), *Paisajes históricos y arqueología medieval*, pp. 233–76. Granada: Alhulia.

Manem, S. (2020). Modeling the evolution of ceramic traditions through a phylogenetic analysis of the Chaînes Opératoires: The European Bronze Age as a case study, *Journal of Archaeological Method and Theory* 27, 992–1039. 10.1007/s10816-019-09434-w.

Mangas, J. & del Rosario Hernando, M. (2011). *La Sal en la Hispania romana*. Madrid: Arco/Libros. Cuadernos de historia 113.

Marc, D. (2006). Sisteme de transport şi de comercializare tradiţională a sării. In V. Cavruc and A. Chiricescu (eds.), *Sarea, Timpul şi Omul*, pp. 152–7. Sfântu Gheorghe: Editura Angustia.

Marcigny, C. & Le Goaziou, E. (2012). Du sel littoral pour conserver et consommer. In A. Lehoërff (ed.), *Beyond the Horizon: Societies of the Channel and North Sea 3,500 years ago*, pp. 101. Paris: Somogy Art Publishers / BOAT 1550 BC.

Marcigny, C., Lemaire, F. & Viau, Y. (2020). Les bouilleurs de sel de l'âge du Bronze. Production et consommation du sel en Europe de l'Ouest, *Bulletin de l'APRAB* Supplément 6, 92–108.

Marro, C. (2010). Where did Late Chalcolithic Chaff-Faced Ware originate? Cultural dynamics in Anatolia and Transcaucasia at the dawn of urban civilization (ca. 4500–3500 BC), *Paléorient* 36/2, 35–55.

Marro, C. (2011). La mine de sel de Duzdaği: une exploitation plurimillénaire, *Mission Archéologique du Bassin de l'Araxe & Academy of Sciences of Azerbaijan, Naxçivan branch (AMEA)*, www.clio.fr/securefilesystem/Marro-Clio2011-texte.doc, accessed 29 April 2013.

Marro, C., Bakhshaliyev, V. & Sanz, S. (2010). Archaeological investigations on the salt mine of Duzdaği (Nakhchivan, Azerbaïdjan), *TÜBA-AR* 13, 229–44.

Martínez Mangato, J. (2012). La producción fenico-púnica de sal en el contexto del Mediterráneo occidental desde una prespectiva diachrónica. In B. Costa and J. H. Fernández (eds.), *Sal, Pesca y Salazones Fenicios en Occidente. XXVI Jornadas de Arqueología Fenicio-Púnica (Eivissa, 2011)*, pp. 9–32. Eivissa: Museu Arqueològic d'Eivissa i Formentera.

Martínez Torrecilla, J. M., Plata Montero, A. & Sánchez Zufiaurre, L. (2013). Paisaje cultural del Valle Salado de Añana. Intervención arqueológica en el extremo sur, *Arkeoikuska* 12, 48–53.

Matthias, W. (1961). Das mitteldeutsche Briquetage – Formen, Verbreitung und Verwendung, *Jahresschrift für mitteldeutsche Vorgeschichte* 45, 119–225.

Matthias, W. (1976). Die Salzproduktion – ein bedeutender Faktor in der Wirtschaft der frühbronzezeitlichen Bevölkerung an der mittleren Saale, *Jahresschrift für mitteldeutsche Vorgeschichte* 60, 373–94.

Maxim, I. A. (1971). Un depozit de unelte dacice pentru exploatarea sării, *Acta Musei Napocensis* 8, 457–63.

Mayer, E. F. (1977). *Die Äxte und Beile in Österreich*. München: Beck. Prähistorische Bronzefunde, Abt. IX, 9.

McKillop, H. (2002). *Salt: White gold of the Ancient Maya*. Gainesville: University Press of Florida.

Meiggs, R. (1973). *Roman Ostia*, 2nd ed. Oxford: Clarendon Press.

Mihailescu-Bîrliba, L. (2016). Les salines en Dacie romaine: remarques sur le personnel administratif, *Studia Antiqua et Archaeologica* 22(1), 51–8.

Miles, A. (1975). Salt-panning in Romano-British Kent. In K. W. de Brisay and K. A. Evans (eds.), *Salt: The study of an ancient industry*, pp. 26–31. Colchester: Colchester Archaeological Group.

Moinier, B. & Weller, O. (2015). *Le Sel dans l'Antiquité, ou Les Cristaux d'Aphrodite*. Paris: Les Belles Lettres.

Moinier, B. (2011). Salt in the antiquity: a quantification essay. In M. Alexianu, O. Weller and R.-G. Curcă (eds.), *Archaeology and Anthropology of Salt:*

A diachronic approach, pp. 137–48. Oxford: Archaeopress. BAR International Series 2198.

Mollat, M. (ed.) (1968). *Le rôle du sel dans l'histoire*. Paris: Presses Universitaires de France.

Montagnari Kokelj, E. (2007). Salt and the Trieste karst (north-eastern Italy). In D. Monah, G. Dumitroaia, O. Weller and J. Chapman (eds.), *L'exploitation du sel à travers le temps*, pp. 161–89. Piatra-Neamţ: Editura Constantin Matasă.

Morelli, C. & Forte, V. (2014). Il *campus salinarum romanarum* e l'epigrafe dei *conductores*: il contesto archeologico, *Mélanges de l'École française de Rome – Antiquité* 126(1), 10–21. https://doi.org/10.4000/mefra.2059.

Morère, N. (2002). À propos du sel hispanique. In O. Weller (ed.), *Archéologie du sel: techniques et sociétés dans la pré- et protohistoire européenne / Salzarchäologie. Techniken und Gesellschaft in der Vor- und Frühgeschichte Europas*, pp. 183–8. Rahden/Westf.: Verlag Marie Leidorf. Internationale Archäologie: Arbeitsgemeinschaft, Symposium, Tagung, Kongress, Band 3.

Morère, N. (2006). Le sel atlantique hispanique dans l'Antiquité. In J.-C. Hocquet and J.-L. Sarrazin (eds.), *Le Sel de la Baie. Histoire, archéologie, ethnologie des sels atlantiques*, pp. 65–85. Rennes: Presses Universitaires de Rennes.

Morin, D. (2002). L'extraction du sel dans les Alpes durant la Préhistoire. La source salée de Moriez, Alpes de Haute Provence (France) (cal. BC 5810–5526). In O. Weller (ed.), *Archéologie du sel: techniques et sociétés dans la pré- et protohistoire européenne / Salzarchäologie. Techniken und Gesellschaft in der Vor- und Frühgeschichte Europas*, pp. 153–62. Rahden/Westf.: Verlag Marie Leidorf.

Morin, D., Lavier, C. & Guiomar, M. (2006). The beginnings of salt extraction in Europe (sixth millennium BC): the salt spring of Moriez (Alpes-de-Haute-Provence, France), *Antiquity* 80 Project Gallery, http://antiquity.ac.uk /ProjGall/morin/index.html, accessed 24 October 2006.

Morris, E. L. (1985). Prehistoric salt distributions: two case studies from western Britain, *Bulletin Board of Celtic Studies* 32, 336–79.

Morris, E. L. (1994). Production and distribution of pottery and salt in Iron Age Britain: a review, *Proceedings of the Prehistoric Society* 60, 371–94.

Multhauf, R. P. (1978). *Neptune's Gift: A history of common salt*. Baltimore: John Hopkins University Press. John Hopkins Studies in the History of Technology, new series 2.

Murolo, N. (1995). Le saline herculeae di Pompei. Produzione del sale e culto di Ercole nella Campania antica, *Studi sulla Campania preromana* 2, 105–22.

Németh, T. G. (2013). Angaben zum spätbronzezeitlichen Salzverkehr. In B. Rezi, R. E. Németh and S. Berecki (eds.), *Bronze Age Crafts and Craftsmen in the Carpathian Basin. Proceedings of the International Colloquium from Târgu Mureş 5–7 October 2012*, pp. 57–63. Târgu Mureş: Editura MEGA.

Nevell, M. & Fielding, A. P. (eds.) (2004–5). Brine in Britannia: recent archaeological work on the Roman salt industry in Cheshire, *Archaeology North West 7* (Issue 17). Council for British Archaeology North West, The Lion Salt Works Trust, & University of Manchester Archaeology Unit.

Nijboer, A. J., Attema, P. A. J. & Van Oortmerssen, G. J. M. (2005–6). Ceramics from a Late Bronze Age saltern on the coast near Nettuno (Rome, Italy), *Palaeohistoria* 47(48), 141–205.

Nikolov, V. (ed.) (2008). *Praistoricheski solodobiven tsentr Provadiya-Solnitsata. Razkopki 2005–2007 g.* Sofia: Bl'garska Akademiya na Naukite / Natsionalen Arkheologicheski Institut i Muzej.

Nikolov, V. (ed.) (2009). *Provadiya-Solnitsata. Arkheologicheski razkopki i izsledvaniya prez 2008 g. Predvaritelen otchet.* Sofia: Publisher not stated.

Olivier, L. & Kovacik, J. (2006). The 'Briquetage de la Seille' (Lorraine, France): proto-industrial salt production in the European Iron Age, *Antiquity* 80, 558–66.

Olivier, L. (2000 (2001)).Le «Briquetage de la Seille» (Moselle): nouvelles recherches sur une exploitation proto-industrielle du sel à l'Age du Fer, *Antiquités nationales* 32, 143–71.

Olivier, L. (2005). Le «Briquetage de la Seille» (Moselle): bilan d'un programme de cinq années de recherches archéologiques (2001–2005), *Antiquités nationales* 37, 219–30.

Olivier, L. (2010). Nouvelles recherches sur le site de sauniers du premier Age du Fer de Marsal '*La Digue*» (Moselle), *Antiquités nationales* 41, 127–60.

Olivier, L. (2015). Iron Age 'proto-industrial' salt mining in the Seille river valley (France): production methods and the social organization of labour. In A. Danielisová and M. Fernández-Götz (eds.), *Persistent Economic Ways of Living: Production, distribution, and consumption in late prehistory and early history*, pp. 69–89. Budapest: Archaeolingua.

Pannuzi, S. (2013). La laguna di Ostia: produzione del sale e trasformazione del paesaggio dall'età antica all'età moderna, *Mélanges de l'École française de Rome – Moyen Âge* 125(2), https://doi.org/10.4000/mefrm.1507.

Pany, D. & Teschler-Nicola, M. (2007). Working in a salt mine: everyday life for the Hallstatt females?, *Lunula* 15, 89–97.

Pasquinucci, M. & Menchelli, S. (2002). The Isola di Coltano Bronze Age village and the salt production in north coastal Tuscany (Italy). In O. Weller (ed.), *Archéologie du sel: techniques et sociétés dans la pré- et protohistoire européenne / Salzarchäologie. Techniken und Gesellschaft in der Vor- und Frühgeschichte Europas*, pp. 177–82. Rahden/Westf.: Marie Leidorf. Internationale Archäologie 3.

Penney, S. & Shotter, D. C. A. (1996). An inscribed Roman salt-pan from Shavington, Cheshire, *Britannia* 27, 360–5.

Pétrequin, P. *et al.* (2001). Salt springs exploitation without pottery during prehistory: from New Guinea to the French Jura. In S. Beyries and P. Pétrequin (eds.), *Ethno-Archaeology and Its Transfers*, pp. 37–65. Oxford: BAR International Series 983.

Pétrequin, P., Pétrequin, A.-M. & Weller, O. (2000). Cuire la pierre et cuire le sel en Nouvelle-Guinée: des techniques actuelles de régulation sociale. In P. Pétrequin, P. Fluzin, J. Thiriot and P. Benoit (eds.), *Arts du feu et productions artisanales*, pp. 545–64. Antibes: Éditions APDCA. XXe Rencontres Internationales d'Archéologie et d'Histoire d'Antibes.

Petzschmann, U. (2015). Salz im Paulusviertel – eine bronze-/eisenzeitliche Siedlung im Stadtgebiet von Halle. In C. Schulz (ed.), *Archäologie findet Stadt: Hallische Stadtgeschichte unter dem Pflaster (Forschungen zur hallischen Stadtgeschichte)*, pp. 43–59. Halle: Verein für Hallische Stadtgeschichte.

Poole, C. (1987). Salt working. In B. Cunliffe (ed.), *Hengistbury Head, Dorset*, vol. 1, pp. 178–80. Oxford: Oxford Committee for Archaeology.

Preisig, E. (1877). Geschichte des Máramaroser Bergbaues, *Oesterreichische Zeitschrift für Berg- und Hüttenwesen* 25/28–30, 301–3, 311–13, 321–3. Tafel 12.

Prilaux, G. (2000). *La production de sel à l'Age du Fer. Contribution à l'établissement d'une typologie à partir des exemples de l'autoroute A16*. Montagnac: éditions monique mergoil. Protohistoire européene 5.

Prilaux, G. *et al.* (2011). Les âges du sel en Gaule du Nord, *Archéopages* 31 (January), 22–31.

Proctor, J. (2012). The Needles Eye enclosure, Berwick-upon-Tweed, *Archaeologia Aeliana* 5th series 41, 19–122.

Querré, G., Cassen, S. & Vigier, E. (eds.) (2019). *La parure en callaïs du Néolithique européen*. Oxford: Archaeopress Publishing.

Quixal Santos, D. (2020). Explotación de la sal, vías de comunicación y territorio durante la Edad del Hierro en el entorno del río Cabriel, *SPAL Revista de Prehistoria y Arqueología de la Universidad de Sevilla* 2(2), 31–48. https://dx.doi.org/10.12795/spal.2020.i29.16.

Rausch, A. W. (2007). Viele Fotos, wenig Platz – Das große Foto-Puzzle von Hallstatt. Fotografische Dokumentation unter Tage. In R. Karl and

J. Leskovar (eds.), *Interpretierte Eisenzeiten: Fallstudien, Methoden, Theorie. Tagungsbeiträge der 2. Linzer Gespräche zur interpretativen Eisenzeitarchäologie*, pp. 109–18. Linz: Oberösterreichisches Landesmuseum. Studien zur Kulturgeschichte von Oberösterreich, Folge 19.

Riehm, K. (1954). Vorgeschichtliche Salzgewinnung an Saale und Seille, *Jahresschrift für mitteldeutsche Vorgeschichte* 38, 112–56.

Riehm, K. (1960). Die Formsalzproduktion der vorgeschichtlichen Salzsiedestätten Europas, *Jahresschrift für mitteldeutsche Vorgeschichte* 44, 180–217.

Riehm, K. (1962). Werkanlagen und Arbeitsgeräte urgeschichtlicher Salzsieder, *Germania* 40, 360–400.

Rippon, S. (2007). *Landscape, Community and Colonisation: The north Somerset levels during the 1st to 2nd millennia AD*. York: Council for British Archaeology. CBA Research Reports 152.

Rodwell, W. J. (1979). Iron Age and Roman salt-winning on the Essex coast. In B. C. Burnham and H. B. Johnson (eds.), *Invasion and Response: The case of Roman Britain*, pp. 133–75. Oxford: British Archaeological Reports 73.

Rouzeau, N. (2002). Sauneries et briquetages. Essai sur la productivité des établissements salicoles gaulois du Centre-Ouest atlantique d'après l'étude du gisement de Nalliers (Vendée). In O. Weller (ed.), *Archéologie du sel: techniques et sociétés dals al Pré- et Protohistoire européenne / Salzarchäologie: Techniken und Gesellschaft in der Vor- und Frühgeschichte Europas*, pp. 99–124. Rahden/Westf.: Marie Leidorf.

Saile, T. (2015). Competing on unequal terms: saltworks at the turn of the Christian era. In R. Brigand and O. Weller (eds.), *Archaeology of Salt: Approaching an invisible past*, pp. 199–209. Leiden: Sidestone.

Saïtas, Y. C. & Zarkia, C. I. (2006). La récolte du sel dans la péninsule du Magne (Péloponnèse). In J.-C. Hocquet and J.-L. Sarrazin (eds.), *Le sel de la Baie. Histoire, archéologie, ethnologie des sels atlantiques*, pp. 349–64 Rennes: Presses universitaires de Rennes.

Sealey, P. R. (1995). New light on the salt industry and Red Hills of prehistoric and Roman Essex, *Essex Archaeology and History* 26, 65–81.

Sevink, J. *et al.* (2020). Protohistoric briquetage at Puntone (Tuscany, Italy): Principles and processes of an industry based on the leaching of saline lagoonal sediments, *Geoarchaeology* 2020, 1–18. https://DOI.org/10.1002/gea.21820.

Sherlock, S. J. (2021). Is there evidence for Neolithic salt manufacture in the UK? The case for Street House, Loftus, North-East England, *Antiquity* 95, 648–69.

Simon, T. (1995). *Salz und Salzgewinnung im nördlichen Baden-Württemberg. Geologie-Technik-Geschichte.* Sigmaringen: Jan Thorbecke Verlag. Forschungen aus Württembergisch Franken, 42.

Simons, A. (1987). Archäologischer Nachweis eisenzeitlichen Salzhandels von der Nordseeküste ins Rheinland, *Archäologische Informationen* 10, 8–14.

Stockinger, U. (2015). The salt of Rome: remarks on the production, trade and consumption in the north-western provinces. In R. Brigand and O. Weller (eds.), *Archaeology of Salt: Approaching an invisible past,* pp. 183–92. Leiden: Sidestone.

Stöllner, T. (1999). *Der prähistorische Salzbergbau am Dürrnberg bei Hallein I. Forschungsgeschichte – Forschungsstand – Forschungsanliegen.* Rahden/ Westf.: Verlag Marie Leidorf. Dürrnberg-Forschungen Band 1, Abteilung Bergbau.

Stöllner, T. (2002). *Der prähistorische Salzbergbau am Dürrnberg bei Hallein II. Die Funde und Befunde der Bergwerksausgrabungen zwischen 1990 und 2000.* Rahden/Westf.: Verlag Marie Leidorf. Dürrnberg-Forschungen Band 3, Abteilung Bergbau; Veröffentlichungen aus dem Deutschen Bergbau-Museum Bochum 113. 2 vols.

Stöllner, T. (2003). The economy of Dürrnberg-bei-Hallein: an Iron Age salt-mining centre in the Austrian Alps, *The Antiquaries Journal* 83, 123–94.

Strang, A. (1997). Explaining Ptolemy's Roman Britain, *Britannia* 28, 1–30.

Tasić, N. (2000). Salt use in the Early and Middle Neolithic of the Balkan Peninsula. In L. Nikolova (ed.), *Technology, Style and Society: Contributions to the innovations between the Alps and the Black Sea in prehistory,* pp. 35–40. Oxford: British Archaeological Reports, International Series 854.

Terán Manrique, J. & Morgado, A. (2011). El aprovechamiento prehistórico de sal en la Alta Andalucía. El caso de Fuente Camacho (Loja, Granada), *Cuadernos de Prehistoria y Arqueología de la Universidad de Granada* 21, 221–49.

Terán Manrique, J. (2011). La producción de sal en la prehistoria de la Península Ibérica: estado de la cuestión, *@rqueología y Territorio* 8, 71–84.

Terán Manrique, J. (2015). Aproximacion a la potencialidad productiva de sal por evaporacion solar en el sistema Iberico durante la Edad del Hierro: propuesta para la modelizacion de potencialidades productivas. In A. Maximiano and E. Cerrillo-Cuenca (eds.), *Arqueología y Tecnologías de Información Espacial: una perspectiva ibero-americana,* pp. 114–30. Oxford: Archaeopress.

Terán Manrique, J. (2017). Sal, monedas, vías y fuentes. La localización de Egelasta: un problema por resolver. In F. C. Cortés, L. J. García-Pulido, L. A. Martínez, E. A. García, A. M. Onorato *et al.* (eds.), *Presente y futuro de los paisajes mineros del pasado: estudios sobre minería, metalurgia y poblamiento, VIII Congreso sobre minería y metalurgia históricas en el sudoeste europeo*, pp. 1–10. Granada: SEDPGYM y Dpto. de Prehistoria y Arqueología de la UGR, Editorial Universidad de Granada.

Tessier, M. (1960). Découverte de gisements préhistoriques aux environs de la Pointe-Saint-Gildas, *Bulletin Société Préhistorique Française* 57, 428–34.

Thoen, H. (1975). Iron Age and Roman salt-making sites on the Belgian coast. In K. W. De Brisay and K. A. Evans (eds.), *Salt: The study of an ancient industry, Report on the salt weekend*, pp. 56–60. Colchester: Colchester Archaeological Group.

Traina, G. (1992). Sale e saline nel Mediterraneo antico, *La Parola del Passato* 266, 363–78.

Ursulescu, N. (1977). Exploatarea sării din saramura în neoliticul timpuriu în lumina descoperirilor de la Solca (jud. Suceava), *Studii și cercetări de istorie veche* 28(3), 307–17.

Valera, A. C. (2017). Salt in the 4th and 3rd Millennia BC in Portugal: Specialization, distribution, and consumption, *Cuaternario y Geomorfología* 31, 105–22. https://doi.org/10.17735/cyg.v31i1-2.53656.

Valiente Cánovas, S. & Ayanagüena Sanz, M. (2005). Cerámicas a mano utilizadas en la producción de la sal en las Salinas de Espartinas (Ciempozuelos, Madrid). In O. Puche Riart and M. Ayarzagüena Sanz (eds.), *Minería y Metalurgia históricas en el Sudoeste Europeo*, pp. 61–70. Madrid: SEDPGYM-SEHA.

Valiente Cánovas, S. & Ramos, P. (2009). Las salinas de Espartinas: un enclave prehistórico dedicado a la explotacíon de la sal. In SEHA (ed.), *La explotacíon histórica de la sal: investigación y puesta en valor. Actas I Congreso Internacional Salinas de Espartinas, Ciempozuelos, 1 y 2 de diciembre de 2006*, pp. 167–82. Madrid: Sociedad Española de Historia de la Arqueología. Memorias de la Sociedad Española de Historia de la Arqueología, II.

Valiente Cánovas, S. *et al.* (2017). Humedales salobres como fuente de extracción de sal en Jerez de la Frontera y su entorno: Cortijo de salinillas y 'Las Salinillas' de Estella del Marqués. In O. Puche Riart, M. Oyarzagüena Sanz, J. F. López Cidád and J. Pous de la Flor (eds.), *Minería y Metalurgias Históricas en el sudoeste europeo. Nuestras raices mineras*, pp. 173–85. Madrid: Sociedad Española para la defensa del Patrimonio Geológico y Minero.

van den Broeke, P. W. (1995). Iron Age sea salt trade in the Lower Rhine area. In J. D. Hill and C. G. Cumberpatch (eds.), *Different Iron Ages: Studies on the*

Iron Age in Temperate Europe, pp. 149–62. Oxford: British Archaeological Reports. BAR International Series 602.

van den Broeke, P. W. (2007). Zoutwinning langs de Noordzee: de pre-middeleeuwse sporen. In A. M. J. de Kraker and G. J. Borger (eds.), *Veen-Vis-Zout. Landschappelijke dynamiek in de zuidwestelijke delta van de Lage Landen*, pp. 65–80. Amsterdam: Vrije Universiteit. Geoarchaeological and Bioarchaeological Studies 8.

von Rauchhaupt, R. & Schunke, T. (2010). *Am Rande des Altsiedellandes – Archäologische Ausgrabungen an der Ortsumgehung Brehna.* Halle/Saale: Landesamt für Denkmalpflege und Archäologie Sachsen-Anhalt / Landesmuseum für Vorgeschichte. Archäologie in Sachsen-Anhalt, Sonderband 12.

Walmsley, J. G. (2000). The ecological importance of Mediterranean salinas. In N. A. Korovessis and T. D. Lekkas (eds.), *SALTWORKS: Preserving Saline Coastal Ecosystems, 6th Conference on Environmental Science and Technology, Pythagorion, Samos, 1 September 1999. Post conference symposium proceedings*, pp. 81–95. Marousi: Global NEST.

Weller, O. (2002). The earliest rock salt exploitation in Europe: a salt mountain in the Spanish Neolithic, *Antiquity* 76, 317–18.

Weller, O. (2012). La production chalcolithique du sel à Provadia-Solnitsata: de la technologie céramique aux implications socio-économiques. In V. Nikolov (ed.), *Salt and Gold: the role of salt in prehistoric Europe*, pp. 67–87. Provadia / Veliko Tarnovo: Verlag Faber.

Weller, O. (2015). First salt making in Europe: An overview from Neolithic times, *Documenta Praehistorica* 42, 185–96.

Weller, O. & Dumitroaia, G. (2005). The earliest salt production in the world: an early Neolithic exploitation in *Poiana Slatinei*-Lunca, Romania, *Antiquity* 79, http://antiquity,ac.uk/ProjGall/weller/index.html, accessed 14 Auguest 2007.

Weller, O. & Figuls, A. (2007). Première exploitation de sel gemme en Europe: organisation et enjeux socio-économiques au Néolithique moyen autour de *La Muntanya de Sal* de Cardona (Catalogne). In A. Figuls and O. Weller (eds.), *1a Trobada internacional d'arqueologia envers l'explotatió de la sal a la prehistòria i protohistòria, Cardona, 6–8 de desembre del 2003*, pp. 219–39. Cardona: Institut de recerques envers la Cultura (IREC).

Weller, O. *et al.* (2008). Première exploitation de sel en Europe. Techniques et gestion de l'exploitation de la source salée de Poiana Slatinei à Lunca (Neamţ, Roumanie). In O. Weller, A. Dufraisse and P. Pétrequin (eds.), *Sel, eau et forêt. D'hier à aujourd'hui*, pp. 205–30. Besançon: Presses universitaires de Franche-Comté. Collection 'Les cahiers de la MSHE Ledoux', 12.

Weller, O. *et al.* (2009). Lunca-Poiana Slatinei (jud. Neamţ): cel mai vechi sit de exploatare a sării din preistoria europeană, *Arheologia Moldovei* 32, 21–39.

Williams, E. (1999). The ethnoarchaeology of salt production at Lake Cuitzeo, Mexico, *Latin American Antiquity* 10, 400–14.

Williams, M. & Reid, M. (2008). *Salt: Life and Industry. Excavations at King Street, Middlewich, Cheshire, 2001–2002.* Oxford: Archaeopress. BAR British Series 456.

Willis, S. (2016). The briquetage containers and salt networks in north-east England. In C. C. Haselgrove (ed.), *Cartimandua's capital? The Late Iron Age royal site at Stanwick, North Yorkshire, fieldwork and analysis, 1981–2011*, pp. 256–61. York: Council for British Archaeology. CBA Research Report 175.

Wollmann, V. (1996). *Mineritul metalifer, extragerea sării şi carierele de piatră în Dacia Romană / Der Erzbergbau, die Salzgewinnung und die Steinbrüche im Römischen Dakien.* Cluj-Napoca: Muzeul Naţional de Istorie a Transilvaniei. Bibliotheca Musei Napocensis 13 / Veröffentlichungen aus dem Deutschen Bergbau-Museum Bochum 63.

Woodiwiss, S. (ed.) (1992). *Iron Age and Roman Salt Production and the Medieval Town of Droitwich.* CBA Research Report 81. London: Council for British Archaeology.

Yoshida, T., translated and revised by Hans Ulrich Vogel (1993). *Salt Production Techniques in Ancient China: The Aobo tu.* Leiden & New York: E.J. Brill.

Acknowledgements

This volume came about through an invitation from Professor Bettina Arnold to contribute to the Elements series being published by Cambridge University Press together with the European Association of Archaeologists. An earlier work of mine (Harding 2013) covered much the same ground as this volume, but at considerably greater length. In seeking to adapt the subject matter to the smaller confines of the Elements series, I have removed most of the more discursive passages that appeared in that work, and have attempted to write a new book, avoiding simply cutting and pasting from the old one. I have been helped in this by the need to cover the rather large quantity of material that has appeared since 2013, as well as to extend the timeframe forward to cover the Greek and Roman periods, with a glance towards medieval salt making.

A number of friends and colleagues have assisted me in the task of bringing the account up to date by drawing my attention to new work, some of it only available in rather (to me) obscure publications from across Europe. I would also like to thank those publishers and authors who gave permission for their illustrations to be used here.

Bettina Arnold was kind enough to read and comment on a complete first draft of the Element. Ian Brown, Brais Currás, Janice Kinory and Tom Lane kindly read individual sections and provided invaluable feedback. I am very grateful to them all.

It is a great pleasure to offer sincere thanks to all those who have helped me in this task, by supplying publications or illustrations, or otherwise providing information (in alphabetical order):

Ian Brown, Jane Burkowski, Dan Buzea, Paola Cassola Guida, Valeriu Cavruc (Valery Kavruk), Rachel Clarke, Maciej Dębiec, Leigh Dodd, Peter Ettel, Maja Grisonić, Elisa Guerra, Leif Hansen, Kristian Kristiansen, Sébastien Manem, Cyril Marcigny, Aleksandra McClain, Emanuela Montagnari Kokelj, Harald Meller, Nuria Morère, Louis Nebelsick, Gabriella Németh, Lorenzo Nigro, Laurent Olivier, Ioana Oltean, Stephen Rippon, Thomas Saile, Paul Sealey, Jan Sevink, Bettina Stoll-Tucker, Leo Webley, Steve Willis.

Cambridge Elements ☰

The Archaeology of Europe

Manuel Fernández-Götz

University of Edinburgh

Manuel Fernández-Götz is Reader in European Archaeology and Head of the Archaeology Department at the University of Edinburgh. In 2016, he was awarded the prestigious Philip Leverhulme Prize. His main research interests are Iron Age and Roman archaeology, social identities and conflict archaeology. He has directed fieldwork projects in Spain, Germany, the United Kingdom and Croatia.

Bettina Arnold

University of Wisconsin-Milwaukee

Bettina Arnold is Full Professor of Anthropology at the University of Wisconsin-Milwaukee and Adjunct Curator of European Archaeology at the Milwaukee Public Museum. Her research interests include the archaeology of alcohol, the archaeology of gender, mortuary archaeology, Iron Age Europe and the history of archaeology.

About the Series

Elements in the Archaeology of Europe is a collaborative publishing venture between Cambridge University Press and the European Association of Archaeologists. Composed of concise, authoritative, and peer-reviewed studies by leading scholars, each volume in this series will provide timely, accurate, and accessible information about the latest research into the archaeology of Europe from the Paleolithic era onwards, as well as on heritage preservation.

E
A   European Association
A   *of* Archaeologists

Cambridge Elements ≡

The Archaeology of Europe

Elements in the Series

Printed in the United States
by Baker & Taylor Publisher Services